easy italian

easy italian

simple recipes for every occasion

maxine clark

RYLAND
PETERS
& SMALL

LONDON NEW YORK

Designer Sarah Fraser
Commissioning Editor Elsa Petersen-Schepelern
Editor Sharon Cochrane
Picture Research Emily Westlake
Production Sheila Smith
Art Director Gabriella Le Grazie
Publishing Director Alison Starling

Index Hilary Bird

First published in the United States in 2005,

This paperback edition published in 2008
by Ryland Peters & Small, Inc.
519 Broadway, 5th Floor
New York, NY 10012
www.rylandpeters.com

10 9 8 7 6 5 4 3

The original hardcover edition is cataloged as follows:

Library of Congress Cataloging-in-Publication Data
Clark, Maxine.
  Easy Italian : simple recipes for every occasion / Maxine Clark.
    p. cm.
  Includes index.
  ISBN 1-84172-950-7
  1. Cookery, Italian. I. Title.
  TX723.C56533 2005
  641.5945–dc22

2005000605

Printed in China

Notes

All spoon measurements are level unless otherwise
specified.

Ingredients for these recipes are available from larger
supermarkets, vegetable markets, healthfood stores,
and delicatessens.

All eggs are medium unless otherwise specified.
Uncooked or partly cooked eggs should not be
served to the very young, the very old, those with
compromised immune systems, or to pregnant women.

Ovens should be preheated to the specified temperature.
If using a convection oven, cooking times should be
reduced according to the manufacturer's instructions.

All the recipes in this book are by Maxine Clark with the
exception of those listed on page 240, which are by
Silvana Franco.

contents

simple, but delicious	6
antipasti and snacks	8
soup	40
risotto	52
pasta and polenta	72
pizzas, tarts, and bread	100
salads, vegetables, and legumes	122

fish	164
meat and poultry	180
sweet things	196
basics	224
index	*236*
credits	*240*

simple, but delicious

I think the reason I fell in love with Italy and Italian food is the relaxed, informal attitude shown towards cooking and entertaining. Any occasion seems to merit a meal that is lovingly prepared, to be shared by all, whether friends or family.

On a recent trip to Sicily, I met some people at a wine tasting who insisted that I join them for a meal the next day. This wasn't anything grand, but two families got together and, like a well-oiled machine, produced a wonderful meal of home-grown and pickled olives, fresh warm ricotta, salame, *pasta con le sarde* (pasta with wild fennel and fresh sardines), crusty semolina bread with their own new olive oil, and their own wine. I took a *cassata* (a chilled sponge cake filled with sweetened ricotta, chocolate, and candied fruit) from their local cake shop for dessert. The meal couldn't have been simpler. These were busy people who, with great ease, produced a banquet from a handful of fresh ingredients.

This is the key to cooking good Italian food—keep it simple and use the best and freshest ingredients. Italian cooking is not complicated, it is the combinations of flavors and textures that make it so approachable. There are no special, elaborate cooking techniques—some dishes are cooked very quickly, retaining the bright fresh flavor of the ingredients, while some are cooked very slowly, releasing hidden depths and tenderizing the toughest cuts of meat to melting softness.

The recipes in this book are easily prepared and perfect for our hectic lifestyles, resulting in food that is both warm and satisfying, and big on flavor. Take it easy with *Easy Italian*!

antipasti and snacks

During the season, asparagus in all its varieties—from purple-tipped, to green, or white (the beloved one)—is often served with egg in some form, especially in the north of Italy. To our taste, asparagus is overcooked in Italy, but this is how they serve it, and I must say, the slightly longer cooking does bring out the flavor. The truffle oil is an optional luxury—you could add some chopped tarragon to the cream instead—but the truffle oil is wonderful.

asparagus *with egg and truffle butter*

Hard-cook the eggs for about 10 minutes, depending upon size. Let cool in cold water, then peel. Cut the eggs in half and remove the yolks. Finely chop the whites and reserve. Mash the yolks with the butter until well blended. Add a drop or two of truffle oil, if using, and season with salt. Cover and keep at room temperature.

Trim the asparagus. Steam it for about 12 minutes until tender. Arrange on 4 warm plates, sprinkle with the chopped egg white, salt, and pepper, then serve with the golden yolk-butter. (The butter can either be spooned on top of the asparagus or served in little dishes to spread onto each mouthful.)

4 free-range eggs

6 tablespoons unsalted butter, softened

a little truffle oil (optional)

1 lb. fresh asparagus

sea salt and freshly ground black pepper

serves 4

This specialty of Genoa in Liguria uses anchovies as a way of adding savory saltiness, just as fish sauce does in Southeast Asian cooking. It doesn't taste overly fishy, but gives the earthy spinach a depth it would not have otherwise. The combination of salt (anchovies) and sweet (dried fruit), coupled with mild, creamy pine nuts in savory dishes is common all over Italy.

spinach *with anchovies and pine nuts*

2½ lb. fresh spinach

½ cup good olive oil

4 anchovy fillets in oil, drained and chopped

3 tablespoons chopped fresh flat-leaf parsley

3 tablespoons dried currants or small raisins, soaked in warm water for 15 minutes

¼ cup pine nuts

freshly grated nutmeg

sea salt and freshly ground black pepper

serves 4

Tear the stems off the spinach, discard the stems, and wash the leaves very well in plenty of cold water to remove any grit and sand. Shake dry in a colander or salad spinner, but leave some water clinging to the leaves.

Put the leaves in a covered saucepan and cook for a few minutes until they wilt. Drain well in a colander but do not squeeze dry—you need large pieces of spinach.

Warm the oil in a large skillet, add the chopped anchovies and parsley, and stir for 2–3 minutes over medium heat until the anchovies dissolve. Add the spinach, drained currants, and pine nuts. Add a good grating of nutmeg, taste, season with salt and pepper to taste, and stir-fry for about 5 minutes until heated through, glossy, and well mixed. Serve immediately.

zucchini and mint fritters

1 ¼ lb. zucchini

finely grated zest of
1 unwaxed lemon

2 tablespoons chopped
fresh mint leaves

oil, for cooking

sea salt and freshly
ground black pepper

lemon wedges, to serve

batter

2 eggs, separated

2 tablespoons olive oil

1 cup beer

1 cup all-purpose flour

sea salt and freshly
ground black pepper

*an electric deep-fryer
(optional)*

serves 4

My favorite way with zucchini! It changes their watery blandness into sweet and crunchy mouthfuls with just a hint of mint. The batter is light and, if fried at the correct temperature, it doesn't absorb any oil at all.

To make the batter, put the egg yolks in a bowl, beat well, then slowly beat in the oil, followed by the beer, then the flour. Season with salt and pepper to taste. Cover and let rest for 1 hour.

Meanwhile, grate the zucchini coarsely, toss with salt, put in a strainer, and let drain for 10 minutes. Rinse well, then pat dry with paper towels. Put them in a bowl, add the lemon zest, mint, salt, and pepper, and stir well.

Just before cooking, put the egg whites, salt, and pepper in a bowl and beat until firm. Gently fold into the batter. Heat the oil to 375°F in a deep-fryer or in a saucepan with a frying basket. Mix the grated zucchini with enough batter to bind them.

Working in batches, slide about 6 small spoonfuls at a time into the hot oil and fry for 2–3 minutes until golden and crisp. Drain the fritters on paper towels, sprinkle with salt, and serve hot with lemon wedges.

Caponata is rather like ratatouille, but much more exotic. There are dozens of variations of this delectable dish from Sicily. It improves with age, so make a big batch and keep it in the refrigerator or preserve it in large jars. It's served as an antipasto, but is delicious with grilled fish or steak. As always in Sicily and in hot weather, serve at room temperature—it tastes much better.

sweet and sour sicilian eggplant stew

4 medium eggplant, cut into bite-size cubes

¼ cup olive oil

1 onion, chopped

2 celery stalks, sliced

12 very ripe large tomatoes, coarsely chopped, or 28 oz. canned chopped tomatoes

1–2 tablespoons salted capers, rinsed well

½ cup best green olives, pitted

2 tablespoons red wine vinegar

2 teaspoons sugar

vegetable oil, for frying

sea salt

to serve

8 oz. fresh ricotta cheese, about 1 cup

toasted chopped almonds

chopped fresh flat-leaf parsley

an electric deep-fryer (optional)

serves 6

Put the eggplant in a colander, sprinkle with salt, and let drain for 30 minutes.

Meanwhile, heat the olive oil in a large saucepan and add the onion and celery. Cook for 5 minutes until softened but not browned, add the tomatoes, then cook for 15 minutes until pulpy. Add the capers, olives, vinegar, and sugar to the sauce and cook for another 15 minutes.

Rinse the eggplant cubes and pat them dry with paper towels.

Heat the vegetable oil in a deep-fryer to 375°F, add the eggplant in batches, and fry until deep golden brown. This may take some time, but cook them thoroughly, because undercooked eggplant is unpleasant. Alternatively, toss the cubes in olive oil, spread them in a roasting pan, and roast at 400°F for about 20 minutes until well browned and tender. Drain well.

Stir the eggplant into the sauce. Taste and adjust the seasoning (this means adding more sugar or vinegar to taste to balance the flavors) Set aside for 30 minutes or preferably overnight to develop the flavors before serving. Serve warm or at room temperature (never refrigerator-cold) in a shallow bowl and top with the ricotta, almonds, and parsley.

Very simple, this dish relies on pan-grilling the eggplant perfectly. There is nothing worse than an undercooked eggplant, so make sure you baste with plenty of oil, and don't let the pan get too hot or the eggplant will burn before they brown—they should gently sizzle. Add a little crushed or chopped garlic to the dressing if you like, but the mint and lemon flavors are quite delicate.

pan-grilled eggplant *with lemon, mint, and balsamic vinegar*

To make the dressing, put the oil, lemon juice and zest, and balsamic vinegar in a bowl and beat well. Add the sugar, salt, and pepper to taste—it should be fairly sweet. Stir in half the mint, then set aside.

Heat a ridged stovetop grill pan until hot or light an outdoor grill and wait for the coals to turn white. Cut each eggplant into 8 thin slices, brush lightly with olive oil, add to the pan or grill, and cook for 2–3 minutes on each side until golden brown and lightly charred. Arrange the slices on a large platter and spoon the dressing over the top. Cover and set aside so that the eggplant absorbs the flavors of the dressing. Sprinkle with the remaining chopped mint and serve.

2 medium eggplant, about 14 oz.

regular olive oil, for basting

dressing

½ cup extra virgin olive oil

finely grated zest and juice of 1 ripe unwaxed lemon

2 tablespoons balsamic vinegar

1–2 teaspoons sugar

¼ cup very coarsely chopped fresh mint leaves

sea salt and freshly ground black pepper

a stovetop grill pan or outdoor grill

serves 4

marinated fresh anchovies

There's nothing quite like these light, fresh, silvery morsels eaten fillet by fillet with a glass of chilled *vino bianco*, overlooking a peacock sea, with a warm salty breeze on your face. If you've never tried a fresh anchovy before, and see them in a market, buy them. They are mild and fresh, and the combination of lemon, parsley, and olive oil is lifted by the zing of scallions.

16 fresh anchovies or small sardines

freshly squeezed juice of 2 lemons

2 fat scallions, thinly sliced

2 tablespoons chopped fresh flat-leaf parsley

extra virgin olive oil

sea salt and freshly ground black pepper

serves 4

To clean the anchovies, cut off the heads and slit open the bellies. Remove the insides (there isn't very much there at all) under running water. Slide your thumb along the backbone to release the flesh along its length. Take hold of the backbone at the head end and lift it out. The fish should now open up like a book. At this stage you can decide whether to cut it into 2 long fillets or leave it whole—size will dictate. Pat them dry with paper towels.

Put the lemon juice in a shallow non-reactive dish and add the anchovies in an even layer, skin side up. Cover and let marinate in the refrigerator for 24 hours.

The next day, lift them out of the lemon juice—they will look pale and "cooked." Arrange them on a serving dish. Sprinkle with the scallions, parsley, and a large quantity of olive oil, season with salt and pepper, and serve at room temperature.

The combination of sweet, salty Parma ham or a local *prosciutto crudo* and a yielding soft fruit like ripe figs or melon is one of life's little miracles. This is an all-time classic, and none the worse for that. I have been served this with a little trickle of aged balsamic vinegar over the figs, which was amazing. If you find a really aged one on your travels, buy it—never mind the expense. It will be thick, sweet, and syrupy, and heaven to use in tiny amounts.

parma ham
with figs and balsamic dressing

4 large or 8 small fresh ripe figs (preferably purple ones)

1 tablespoon good balsamic vinegar

extra virgin olive oil, for brushing and serving

12 thin slices of Parma ham or prosciutto

6 oz. fresh Parmesan cheese, broken into craggy lumps

crushed black pepper, to serve

serves 4

Take each fig and stand it upright. Using a sharp knife, make 2 cuts across each fig not quite quartering it, but keeping it intact. Ease the figs open and brush with balsamic vinegar and olive oil.

Arrange 3 slices of Parma ham on each plate with the figs and Parmesan on top. Sprinkle with extra virgin olive oil and plenty of crushed black pepper.

A wonderful explosion of the flavors of sage and anchovy through crisp batter. These must be served virtually straight out of the pan. You could use a package of Japanese tempura batter for this—it is so light and crisp.

deep-fried sage leaves

24 large fresh sage leaves

1 teaspoon salted capers, rinsed

1 tablespoon anchovy paste

vegetable oil, for deep-frying

batter

1 egg

²/₃ cup ice water

1 cup all-purpose flour

makes 12

Wash and dry the sage leaves. Mash the capers with the anchovy paste and spread onto the darker green sides of 12 of the leaves. Press another leaf on top of the filling to form a sandwich.

To make the batter, lightly beat the egg and the ice water together. Add the flour and beat again, leaving the mixture a bit lumpy. Do not let it stand.

Heat the oil in a deep pan or wok until a piece of stale bread turns golden in a few seconds when dropped in. Holding the leaves by the stems, dip them into the batter, and lightly shake off the excess. Place into the hot oil, a few at a time, and fry until crisp and barely golden. This will only take a few seconds. Drain on paper towels and serve immediately.

These are a great example of Sicilian street food—little fritters made out of ground chickpeas. So popular throughout the Mediterranean, every country has a form of snack made with these versatile legumes. The fritters are crisp on the outside and soft in the middle. To taste their best they must be served hot and sprinkled with lots of sea salt.

sicilian chickpea and rosemary fritters

2 1/2 cups chickpea flour*, about 11 oz.

3 cups water

1—2 tablespoons chopped fresh rosemary

vegetable oil, for deep-frying

sea salt and freshly ground black pepper

makes about 40

Chickpea flour is known as gram flour in Indian grocery stores, and is also known as besan

Lightly oil a cold surface such as a marble slab or the back of a large baking tray. Have a spatula at the ready! Sift the chickpea flour into a saucepan. Beat in the water slowly, making sure there are no lumps. Stir in the rosemary, and salt and pepper to taste. Bring to a boil, beating all the time, until the mixture really thickens and leaves the side of the pan (like choux pastry). Don't worry if you get lumps at this stage, they will disappear when you fry the fritters.

Now you need to work really quickly. Tip the mixture onto the oiled surface and spread it out as thinly and evenly as you can—aim to make it about 1/8-inch thick. Let cool and set.

When set, cut into small triangles or squares. To prevent them drying out, place them between layers of plastic wrap until ready to cook. Heat some oil in a wok or deep-fryer. The oil is ready when a piece of mixture will sizzle instantly when dropped in. Deep-fry a few fritters at a time, turning when golden brown. Drain on paper towels and sprinkle with salt. Serve hot.

traditional peasant tomato and garlic bruschetta

This is called *fettunta* in Italy, a word that comes from the Tuscan dialect and derives from Latin, meaning "anointed slice." It is a slice of bread grilled over hot coals, rubbed with garlic, and sprinkled with olive oil. To be authentic you should use only the finest Tuscan extra virgin olive oil. The ripe tomato is just crushed in your hand and smashed onto the bread, then eaten immediately. This is bruschetta at its simplest and best. Here is a more civilized version, but you should try the real thing.

Coarsely chop the tomatoes and season with salt and pepper.

To make the bruschetta, broil, toast, or pan-grill the bread on both sides until lightly browned or toasted. Rub the top side of each slice with the cut garlic, then sprinkle with olive oil.

Spoon the tomatoes over the bruschetta and sprinkle with more olive oil. Eat immediately with your fingers!

4 large very ripe tomatoes

4 thick slices of country bread, preferably sourdough

2 garlic cloves, cut in half

extra virgin olive oil, for sprinkling

sea salt and freshly ground black pepper

serves 4

This is pared-down simplicity and so easy to make. It beats the likes of doughballs and garlic bread hands down. The most important thing is not to overcook the garlic—it must on no account turn brown. This is great served instead of garlic bread, with a selection of salads.

olive oil and garlic bruschetta

4 large garlic cloves

⅓ cup extra virgin olive oil

a good pinch hot red pepper flakes

¼ cup chopped fresh flat-leaf parsley (optional)

4 thick slices of country bread, preferably sourdough

serves 4

Slice the garlic lengthwise into paper-thin slices. Heat the olive oil in a small saucepan and stir in the garlic. Cook until the garlic starts to give off its aroma and is golden but not brown (or it will taste bitter). Remove the pan from the heat, then mix in the hot red pepper flakes and parsley, if using. Cover to keep warm.

To make the bruschetta, broil, toast, or pan-grill the bread on both sides until lightly browned or toasted. Spoon or brush over the garlicky oil. Eat immediately with your fingers!

artichoke, pesto, and pine nut bruschetta

This is a joy to make when fresh artichokes are in season. The pesto and pine nuts are perfect foils for the slightly bitter taste of the artichoke. If fresh ones are unavailable, you can use canned artichokes or those preserved in oil. Whichever you use, lightly fry them to bring out their flavor.

To make the bruschetta, broil, toast, or pan-grill the bread on both sides until lightly browned or toasted. Rub the top side of each slice with the cut garlic, then sprinkle with olive oil. Keep them warm in a low oven.

Prepare the artichoke hearts* and cut them in half. Heat the oil and butter in a skillet, add the artichoke hearts, and fry gently until they are completely tender and beginning to brown. Add the balsamic vinegar, turn up the heat, and toss the artichoke hearts until the vinegar evaporates.

To make the pesto Genovese, put the garlic, pine nuts, Parmesan, basil leaves, olive oil, and salt and pepper in a blender or food processor and blend until smooth.

Spread the pesto over the bruschetta and divide the artichoke hearts between the slices. Sprinkle with the pine nuts and Parmesan shavings. Serve immediately.

*Note To prepare fresh artichoke hearts, fill a bowl with water and squeeze in the juice of ½ lemon. Use the other lemon half to rub the cut portions of the artichokes as you work. Trim the artichokes by snapping off the dark green outer leaves, starting at the bottom. Trim the stalk to about 2 inches and peel it. Cut about ½ inch off the tip of each artichoke heart, then put them in the lemony water, to stop them discoloring, until required.

4 thick slices of country bread, preferably sourdough

2 garlic cloves, cut in half

extra virgin olive oil, for brushing

artichoke topping

6 small, fresh artichokes, each about 3 inches long

2 tablespoons olive oil

2 tablespoons butter

1 tablespoon balsamic vinegar

pesto genovese

2 garlic cloves

½ cup pine nuts, about 2 oz.

¼ cup freshly grated Parmesan cheese

1½ cups fresh basil leaves

⅔ cup extra virgin olive oil

sea salt and freshly ground black pepper

to serve

2 tablespoons pine nuts, toasted

shavings of Parmesan cheese

serves 4

This is a very popular combination of ingredients in southern Italy. Sweet shrimp and tomatoes contrast with earthy chickpeas, pungent garlic, and a hint of fiery chile. Great food for warm summer evenings outdoors.

spicy garlic shrimp *with tomatoes and chickpeas on bruschetta*

Heat the oil in a large skillet and add the garlic, fry until just turning golden (do not let it burn), then add the hot red pepper flakes and wine. Turn up the heat and boil on high to reduce the wine to almost nothing. Add the tomatoes (if you are using canned tomatoes, add some sugar to bring out their flavor) and cook for 1–2 minutes until they start to soften. Stir in the shrimp and chickpeas and bring to a boil. Simmer for 2–3 minutes, then stir in the parsley and season with salt and pepper to taste. Set aside.

To make the bruschetta, broil, toast, or pan-grill the bread on both sides until lightly browned or toasted. Rub the top side of each slice with the cut garlic, then sprinkle with olive oil. Spoon the shrimp mixture on top and serve immediately.

2 tablespoons extra virgin olive oil, plus extra for sprinkling

2 garlic cloves, finely chopped

½ teaspoon hot red pepper flakes

½ cup dry white wine

½ lb. ripe tomatoes, peeled and chopped, or canned tomatoes, chopped, 1¼–1½ cups

½ teaspoon sugar (optional)

½ lb. raw, shelled shrimp, about 2 cups

½ cup canned chickpeas, rinsed and drained, about 2 oz.

2 tablespoons chopped fresh flat-leaf parsley

4 thick slices of country bread, preferably sourdough

2 garlic cloves, cut in half

sea salt and freshly ground black pepper

serves 4

grilled fig and prosciutto bruschetta *with arugula*

4 thick slices of country bread, preferably sourdough

2 garlic cloves, cut in half

extra virgin olive oil, for sprinkling and brushing

8 ripe fresh figs

2 tablespoons balsamic vinegar

12 slices of prosciutto

1 cup arugula

sea salt and freshly ground black pepper

shavings of Parmesan cheese, to serve

serves 4

This combination of caramelized figs and crisply barbecued prosciutto is irresistible. The figs are best cooked on a grill, but you can use a stovetop grill pan or a broiler—just get the right amount of browning on the figs.

To make the bruschetta, broil, toast, or pan-grill the bread on both sides until lightly browned or toasted. Rub the top side of each slice with the cut garlic, then sprinkle with olive oil. Keep in a warm oven.

Take the figs and stand them upright. Using a small, sharp knife, make two cuts across each fig not quite quartering it, but keeping it intact at the base. Ease the figs open and brush with balsamic vinegar and olive oil. Put the figs, cut side down, on a preheated barbecue or stovetop grill pan and cook for 3–4 minutes until hot and slightly browned—don't move them during cooking. Alternatively, place the figs, cut side up, under a really hot broiler until browning and heated through.

While the figs are cooking, place half the slices of prosciutto on the barbecue or stovetop grill pan, or under the broiler, and cook until frazzled. Remove and keep warm while cooking the remaining slices. Place two figs, three pieces of prosciutto, and some arugula on each slice of bruschetta. Cover with Parmesan shavings and sprinkle with olive oil. Season to taste with salt and pepper and serve immediately.

mozzarella in carrozza

This is a classic Italian restaurant favorite, but this more rustic version is so easy to make at home. The mozzarella melts inside the crisp bread coat, revealing a surprise of sun-dried tomatoes and anchovies inside.

18 oz. mozzarella cheese, thickly sliced

8 thin oval slices of country bread

8 sun-dried tomatoes, soaked until soft and cut into strips

8 anchovy fillets in oil, drained

2 teaspoons dried oregano

3 eggs, beaten

vegetable oil, for shallow frying

sea salt and freshly ground black pepper

serves 4

Arrange the mozzarella slices over 4 of the slices of bread. Sprinkle the sun-dried tomatoes, anchovy fillets, and oregano over the mozzarella. Season well with salt and pepper, then put the remaining bread slices on top to make sandwiches. Press down well.

Pour the beaten eggs into a large dish and dip the sandwiches in them, turning once to coat both sides. Leave them in the egg for 30 minutes to soak it up.

Heat the oil in a deep skillet until a crumb dropped in sizzles instantly. Fry each sandwich for 1–2 minutes on each side until crisp and golden brown. Drain on paper towels and serve piping hot.

soup

Pappa al pomodoro is only as good as its ingredients—great tomatoes, good bread, and wonderful, green (preferably Tuscan) olive oil. This is one of the most comforting soups on earth and of course has its origins in peasant thrift. Leftover bread is never thrown away in Tuscany—there is always a use for it. Here, it thickens a rich tomato soup, which is in turn enriched with Parmesan.

creamy tomato and bread soup *with basil oil*

6 cups chicken, meat, or Vegetable Broth (page 234)

¼ cup olive oil

1 onion, chopped

2½ lb. very ripe, soft tomatoes, coarsely chopped, about 6½ cups

10 oz. stale white bread, thinly sliced, crusts removed (or about 6 cups bread crumbs)

3 garlic cloves, crushed

1¼ cups freshly grated Parmesan cheese, plus extra to serve

sea salt and freshly ground black pepper

basil oil
⅓ cup chopped fresh basil leaves

⅔ cup extra virgin olive oil

serves 6

Heat the broth slowly in a large saucepan. Meanwhile, heat the oil in another large saucepan, add the onion and tomatoes, and sauté over gentle heat for about 10 minutes until soft. Push the mixture through a food mill or strainer, and stir into the hot broth. Add the bread and garlic.

Cover and simmer gently for about 45 minutes until thick and creamy, beating from time to time to break up the bread. Take care, because this soup can catch on the bottom.

Meanwhile, to make the basil oil, put the basil and olive oil in a blender and blend until completely smooth—if not, pour through a fine wire mesh strainer.

To finish, stir the Parmesan into the soup, then add salt and pepper to taste. Ladle into bowls and trickle 2 tablespoons basil oil over each serving. Serve hot, warm, or cold (but never chilled), with more Parmesan served separately.

la ribollita

1½ cups dried cannellini beans
or other white beans

⅔ cup extra virgin olive oil, plus
extra for serving

1 onion, finely chopped

1 carrot, chopped

1 celery stalk, chopped

2 leeks, finely chopped

4 garlic cloves, finely chopped,
plus 1 extra peeled and bruised,
for rubbing

1 small white cabbage,
thinly sliced

1 large potato, chopped

4 medium zucchini, chopped

1¾ cups tomato passata
(strained, crushed tomatoes)

2 sprigs of rosemary

2 sprigs of thyme

a handful of fresh sage leaves

1 dried red chile

1 lb. *cavolo nero* (Tuscan black
cabbage) or Savoy cabbage,
thinly sliced

6 thick slices of coarse crusty
white bread

sea salt and freshly ground
black pepper

freshly grated Parmesan cheese,
to serve

serves 8 generously

There's nothing quite like a huge plate of thick, warming *ribollita* on a damp fall evening beside a crackling, scented log fire. Best made in large quantities, this is a great soup for a family get-together and is very filling. *Ribollita* means "reboiled," and is made from whatever vegetables are around, but must contain beans and the delicious Tuscan black winter cabbage, *cavolo nero*. The basic bean and vegetable soup is made the day before, then reheated and ladled over toasted garlic bread, sprinkled with olive oil, and served with lots of Parmesan cheese.

Put the beans in a bowl, cover with cold water, soak overnight, then drain just before you're ready to use them.

Next day, heat half the olive oil in a large, heavy saucepan and add the onion, carrot, and celery. Cook gently for 10 minutes, stirring frequently. Add the leeks and garlic and cook for 10 minutes. Add the white cabbage, potato, and zucchini, stir well, and cook for 10 minutes, stirring frequently.

Stir in the soaked beans, passata, rosemary, thyme, sage, dried chile, salt, and plenty of black pepper. Cover with about 2 quarts water (the vegetables should be well covered), bring to a boil, then turn down the heat and simmer, covered, for at least 2 hours, until the beans are very soft.

Take out 2–3 large ladles of soup and mash well. Stir back into the soup to thicken it. Stir in the cavolo nero or Savoy cabbage and simmer for another 15 minutes.

Remove from the heat, let cool, then refrigerate overnight. The next day, slowly reheat the soup and stir in the remaining olive oil. Toast the bread and rub with garlic. Pile the bread in a tureen or in individual bowls and ladle the soup over the top. Trickle in more olive oil and serve with plenty of freshly grated Parmesan.

spinach broth *with egg and cheese*

1 ½ lb. fresh spinach

4 tablespoons butter

4 eggs

⅓ cup freshly grated
Parmesan cheese

¼ teaspoon freshly
grated nutmeg

about 7 cups good
chicken broth

sea salt and freshly ground
black pepper

serves 6

A typical way to thicken and enrich a broth in many parts of Italy is to add beaten eggs. This is one of the best I have tasted because of the freshness of the greens. Although most of us are limited to spinach, there are many more varieties of *ortaggi* (greens) in Italian markets—beet greens, for example, or even zucchini leaves and tendrils.

Remove all the stalks from the spinach, then wash the leaves thoroughly—do not shake dry. Cook the leaves in a large saucepan with the water still clinging. When the leaves have wilted, drain well, then chop finely.

Heat the butter in a medium saucepan, then add the spinach, tossing well to coat with the butter. Remove from the heat and let cool for 5 minutes.

Put the eggs, Parmesan, nutmeg, salt, and pepper in a bowl and beat well. Mix into the spinach. Put the broth in a large saucepan and bring almost to a boil. When almost boiling, beat in the spinach and egg mixture as quickly as you can to avoid separating. Reheat gently for a couple of minutes, but don't let the broth boil. Serve immediately.

A lovely soup to serve in the summer when fresh peas and mint are plentiful. *Vialone nano* is the favorite risotto rice in the Veneto region. It is a *semi-fino* round-grain rice, best for soups and risotto, but arborio (a *superfino* used mainly for risotto) will do very nicely. This dish has very ancient roots, and was flavored with fennel seeds at one time. Parsley is the usual addition now, but I prefer mint in the summer.

venetian pea and rice soup *with mint*

Put the broth in a large saucepan and bring it slowly to a boil while you prepare the *soffrito* (sautéed sauce).

Heat the olive oil and half of the butter in a large saucepan and, when melted, add the pancetta and scallion. Cook for about 5 minutes until softened but not browned.

Pour in the rice, stir for a few minutes to toast it, then add all the boiling broth. Simmer for 10 minutes, stirring from time to time, then add the peas, and cook for 5–7 minutes. Stir in the remaining butter, mint, and Parmesan. Add salt and pepper to taste and serve immediately. The rice grains should not be too mushy, and the soup should be thick, but not stodgy.

5 cups chicken, beef, or Vegetable Broth (see page 234)

2 tablespoons olive oil

4 tablespoons butter

2 oz. pancetta, finely chopped, about 1/2 cup

1 large scallion (*cipolloto*), or the white parts of 4 scallions, finely chopped

1 cup risotto rice, preferably *vialone nano*

2 1/2 lb. fresh peas in the pod, shelled, or 2 1/2 cups frozen peas

3 tablespoons chopped fresh mint leaves

freshly grated Parmesan cheese

sea salt and freshly ground black pepper

serves 4

Italy produces the most wonderful, comforting soups and this one from Campania combines two of the great stand-bys—beans and pasta. This one is sure to bring a smile of nostalgia to the face of any homesick Italian, probably because it will remind them of *nonna's* version.

pasta and bean soup

1 ¼ cups dried cannellini, navy beans, or other white beans

a pinch of baking soda

¼ cup olive oil, plus extra to serve

2 garlic cloves, crushed

7 cups chicken broth or water

1 cup short pasta shapes, such as *maccheroni* or *tubetti*

4 tomatoes, peeled, seeded, and coarsely chopped

¼ cup chopped fresh flat-leaf parsley

sea salt and freshly ground black pepper

serves 6

Put the beans in a bowl, cover with cold water, add a pinch of baking soda and soak overnight. The next day, drain the beans just before you're ready to use them.

The next day, put the drained beans in a large saucepan. Add the olive oil, garlic, and broth or water. Bring to to a boil, reduce the heat, and simmer, partially covered with a lid, for 1–2 hours or until the beans are tender.

Working in batches if necessary, blend the beans with the cooking liquid using a blender or food processor. Return the bean puree to the rinsed-out pan, adding extra water or broth as necessary. Add the pasta and simmer gently for 15 minutes until tender. (Add a little extra water or broth if the soup is looking too thick.) Stir in the tomatoes and parsley and season well with salt and pepper. Serve the soup with an extra trickle of olive oil.

risotto

When you have nothing except risotto rice in the pantry, and a chunk of Parmesan and some butter in the refrigerator, yet feel the need for comfort and luxury, this is the risotto for you. It is pale, golden, smooth, and creamy and relies totally on the quality of these few ingredients. I would use real sweet, nutty Parmigiano Reggiano, and nothing else.

parmesan and butter risotto

about 6 cups hot chicken broth or Vegetable Broth (page 234)

1 stick plus 3 tablespoons unsalted butter

1 onion, finely chopped

2 1/3 cups risotto rice, preferably *carnaroli*

2/3 cup dry white wine

1 cup freshly grated Parmesan cheese

sea salt and freshly ground black pepper

serves 4–6

Put the broth in a saucepan and keep at a gentle simmer. Melt half the butter in a large, heavy saucepan and add the onion. Cook gently for 10 minutes until soft, golden, and translucent but not browned. Add the rice and stir until well coated with the butter and heated through. Pour in the wine and boil hard until it has reduced and almost disappeared. This will remove the taste of raw alcohol.

Begin adding the broth, a large ladle at a time, stirring gently until each ladle has almost been absorbed by the rice. The risotto should be kept at a bare simmer throughout cooking, so don't let the rice dry out—add more broth as necessary. Continue until the rice is tender and creamy, but the grains still firm. (This should take 15–20 minutes depending upon the type of rice used—check the package instructions.)

Taste and season well with salt and pepper, then stir in the remaining butter and all the Parmesan. Cover and let rest for a couple of minutes so the risotto can relax and the cheese melt, then serve immediately. You may like to add a little more broth just before you serve, but don't let the risotto wait around too long or the rice will turn mushy.

When you dip your fork into this risotto, you will come across pockets of melting mozzarella. Mix in the tomato topping and you will make more strings. Try to use *mozzarella di bufala*—it has a fresh, lactic bite well-suited to this recipe.

mozzarella and sun-blushed
tomato risotto *with basil*

about 6 cups hot chicken broth or Vegetable Broth (page 234)

1 stick unsalted butter

1 onion, finely chopped

2 cups risotto rice

²/₃ cup dry white wine

8 oz. mozzarella cheese balls, cut into ¹/₂-inch cubes

¹/₄ cup chopped fresh basil leaves, plus extra to serve (optional)

10 oz. sun-blushed tomatoes*

sea salt and freshly ground black pepper

freshly grated Parmesan cheese, to serve

serves 4

*If you are unable to find sun-blushed tomatoes, buy 1 lb. organic grape tomatoes and semi-dry them in a preheated oven at 250°F for about 1 hour

Put the broth in a saucepan and keep at a gentle simmer. Melt half the butter in a large, heavy saucepan and add the onion. Cook gently for 10 minutes until soft, golden, and translucent but not browned. Add the rice and stir until well coated with the butter and heated through. Pour in the wine and boil hard until it has reduced and almost disappeared. This will remove the taste of raw alcohol.

Begin adding the broth, a large ladle at a time, stirring gently until each ladle has been almost absorbed by the rice. The risotto should be kept at a bare simmer throughout cooking, so don't let the rice dry out—add more broth as necessary. Continue until the rice is tender and creamy, but the grains still firm. (This should take 15–20 minutes depending upon the type of rice used—check the package instructions.)

Taste and season well with salt and pepper, then beat in the remaining butter. You may like to add a little more hot broth at this stage to loosen the risotto. Fold in the cubed mozzarella and chopped basil. Cover and let rest for a couple of minutes so the risotto can relax and the cheese melt. Carefully ladle into warm bowls and put a pile of tomatoes in the center of each one. Top with basil leaves and serve immediately with a bowl of grated Parmesan.

wild mushroom risotto

6 cups hot chicken broth or Vegetable Broth (page 234)

1 stick unsalted butter

1 large onion, finely chopped

2 garlic cloves, finely chopped

3 cups mixed wild mushrooms, cleaned and coarsely chopped (or a mixture of wild and fresh, or 1 1/2 cups cultivated mushrooms, plus 1 oz. dried porcini soaked in warm water for 20 minutes, drained and chopped)

1 tablespoon chopped fresh thyme

1 tablespoon chopped fresh marjoram

2/3 cup dry white wine or vermouth

2 1/3 cups risotto rice

3/4 cup freshly grated Parmesan cheese, plus extra to serve

sea salt and freshly ground black pepper

serves 6

We make this risotto in our cooking classes in Tuscany in October, when fresh porcini mushrooms are around. Any fresh wild mushroom will taste wonderful, but it can be made very successfully using a mixture of cultivated mushrooms and reconstituted dried Italian porcini.

Put the broth in a saucepan and keep at a gentle simmer. Melt the butter in a large, heavy saucepan and add the onion and garlic. Cook gently for 10 minutes until soft, golden, and translucent but not browned. Stir in the mushrooms and herbs, then cook over medium heat for 3 minutes to heat through. Pour in the wine and boil hard until it has reduced and almost disappeared. This will remove the taste of raw alcohol. Stir in the rice and sauté with the onion and mushrooms until dry and slightly opaque.

Begin adding the broth, a large ladle at a time, stirring until each ladle has been almost absorbed by the rice. The risotto should be kept at a bare simmer throughout cooking, so don't let the rice dry out—add more broth as necessary. Continue until the rice is tender and creamy, but the grains still firm. (This should take about 15–20 minutes depending upon the type of rice used—check the package instructions.)

Taste and season well with salt and pepper. Stir in the Parmesan, cover, let rest for a couple of minutes, then serve immediately with extra grated Parmesan.

about 6 cups hot chicken broth or Vegetable Broth (page 234)

1 stick unsalted butter

6 scallions, finely chopped

2 garlic cloves, finely chopped

1¼ cups cubed carrots or a bunch of tiny new carrots, trimmed and scraped but kept whole

2 cups risotto rice, preferably *carnaroli*

4 oz. asparagus spears, trimmed and cut into 1-inch lengths, about 1 cup

¾ cup thin green beans, cut into 1-inch lengths

⅓ cup fresh or frozen peas or fava beans, thawed if frozen

½ cup freshly grated Parmesan cheese, plus extra to serve

⅓ cup chopped mixed fresh herbs, such as chives, dill, flat-leaf parsley, mint, chervil, and tarragon

sea salt and freshly ground black pepper

serves 4

The charm of this risotto is found in the delicate flavors and colors of spring. The vegetables are small and sweet, the herbs fresh and fragrant. Don't be tempted to skimp on the herbs here—as well as imparting intense flavor, they add a beautiful touch of spring green. Sometimes I blend them with the remaining butter (melted) to give a bright green liquid to beat in at the end.

spring risotto *with herbs*

Put the broth in a saucepan and keep at a gentle simmer. Melt half the butter in a large, heavy saucepan and add the scallions, garlic, and carrots. Cook gently for 5 minutes until the scallions are soft and translucent but not browned. Add the rice and stir until well coated with the butter and heated through.

Begin adding the broth, a large ladle at a time, stirring gently until each ladle has been almost absorbed by the rice. The risotto should be kept at a bare simmer throughout cooking, so don't let the rice dry out— add more broth as necessary. After 10 minutes, add the asparagus, beans, and peas, and continue until the vegetables are tender and the rice is tender and creamy, but the grains still firm. (This should take 15–20 minutes depending upon the type of rice used—check the package instructions.)

Taste and season well with salt and pepper, then stir in the remaining butter, the Parmesan, and the herbs. Cover and let rest for a couple of minutes, then serve immediately with extra freshly grated Parmesan cheese. You may like to add a little more hot broth to the risotto just before you serve to loosen it, but don't let it wait around too long or the rice will turn mushy.

A dish from the Veneto, where *vialone nano* rice is grown, as well as several varieties of radicchio. Stirring in a spoonful of mascarpone or cream at the end enriches the risotto and adds sweetness. The risotto has both a sweet and a bitter flavor. I like to add a few currants plumped up for 20 minutes in warm grappa for an added surprise.

creamy radicchio
and mascarpone risotto

about 6 cups hot chicken broth or Vegetable Broth (page 234)

1 stick unsalted butter

2 carrots, finely chopped

½ cup smoked pancetta or prosciutto, finely chopped

2 garlic cloves, finely chopped

1 lb. radicchio, finely shredded

2⅓ cups risotto rice

2 tablespoons currants soaked in ¼ cup warm grappa for 20 minutes (optional)

3 tablespoons mascarpone cheese or heavy cream

¾ cup freshly grated Parmesan cheese, plus extra to serve

sea salt and freshly ground black pepper

serves 6

Put the broth in a saucepan and keep at a gentle simmer. Melt half the butter in a large, heavy saucepan and add the carrots. Cook gently for 5 minutes until softening. Add the pancetta and garlic, and cook for 4 minutes until just beginning to brown. Stir in the radicchio and cook for 4 minutes until it begins to wilt. Add the rice and stir until heated through.

Begin adding the broth, a large ladle at a time, stirring gently until each ladle has been almost absorbed by the rice. The risotto should be kept at a bare simmer throughout cooking, so don't let the rice dry out—add more stock as necessary. Continue adding the broth, ladle by ladle, until the rice is tender and creamy, but the grains still firm. (This should take 15–20 minutes depending upon the type of rice used—check the package instructions).

Taste and season well with salt and plenty of pepper. Add the soaked currants, if using, and stir in the remaining butter, the mascarpone or cream, and the Parmesan. Cover and let rest for a couple of minutes, then serve immediately with extra grated Parmesan.

An amazing risotto to serve on its own as a first course or to accompany meat or game dishes. This risotto needs the sweetness of the vegetables to balance the acidity from the wine. Use a good wine that you would not be ashamed to drink, and you will achieve perfect results. Use a cheap, undrinkable wine and the risotto will be inedible.

red wine risotto

about 6 cups hot chicken broth or Vegetable Broth (page 234)

1 stick unsalted butter

1 small red onion, finely chopped

1 small carrot, finely chopped

1 small celery stalk, finely chopped

3 tablespoons pancetta or prosciutto, finely chopped (optional)

2⅓ cups risotto rice

1¼ cups full-bodied red wine, such as Barolo

1¼ cups freshly grated Parmesan cheese

sea salt and freshly ground black pepper

chopped fresh parsley, to serve

serves 4–6

Put the broth in a saucepan and keep at a gentle simmer. Melt half the butter in a large, heavy saucepan and add the onion, carrot, and celery. Cook gently for 10 minutes until soft, golden, and translucent but not browned. Add the pancetta, if using, and cook for another 2 minutes. Add the rice and stir until well coated with the butter and heated through. Pour in the wine and boil hard until it has been reduced by half. This will remove the taste of raw alcohol.

Begin adding the broth, a large ladle at a time, stirring gently until each ladle has almost been absorbed by the rice. The risotto should be kept at a bare simmer throughout cooking, so don't let the rice dry out—add more broth as necessary. Continue until the rice is tender and creamy, but the grains still firm. (This should take 15–20 minutes depending upon the type of rice used—check the package instructions.)

Taste and season well with salt and pepper, then beat in the remaining butter and all the Parmesan. Cover and let rest for a couple of minutes so the risotto can relax, then serve immediately. You may like to add a little more hot broth to the risotto just before you serve to loosen it, but don't let it wait around too long or the rice will turn mushy. Serve sprinkled with parsley.

Central and northern Italy are the places to go for good risotto—I've never eaten a good one in the south. Seafood risotto should be creamy and slightly soupy. Generally, you will never be offered Parmesan with a fish risotto (except perhaps squid ink risotto)—it is frowned upon, so don't ask!

seafood and saffron risotto

1 teaspoon saffron threads

6 cups light fish broth

1¼ cups dry white wine

12 oz. raw, shelled shrimp, 2½–3 cups

6 baby squid, cleaned and cut into rings

6 fresh scallops, cut in half horizontally if large

1 lb. fresh mussels, cleaned (if unavailable, use extra clams)

8 oz. fresh cherrystone clams, rinsed

3 tablespoons olive oil

1 onion, finely chopped

2½ cups risotto rice, such as *arborio*

sea salt and freshly ground black pepper

3 tablespoons chopped fresh flat-leaf parsley, to serve

serves 6

Put the saffron in a small bowl and cover with boiling water. Set aside to infuse while you cook the fish. Pour the broth and wine into a large saucepan and heat to simmering point. Add the shrimp and cook for 2 minutes. Add the squid and scallops and cook for another 2 minutes. Remove them with a slotted spoon and set aside.

Put the mussels and clams into the broth and bring to a boil. Cover and cook for 3–5 minutes or until all the shells have opened. Remove with a slotted spoon and set aside. Discard any that haven't opened. Keep the broth at a gentle simmer.

Heat the oil in a large, heavy saucepan and add the onion. Cook gently for 10 minutes until the onion is soft and translucent but not browned. Stir in the rice until well coated with the oil and heated through.

Begin adding the broth, a large ladle at a time, stirring gently until each ladle has been almost absorbed by the rice. Add the saffron water with the first ladle. The risotto should be kept at a bare simmer throughout cooking, so don't let the rice dry out—add more broth as necessary. Continue adding the broth, ladle by ladle, until all but 2 ladles of broth remain, and the rice is tender and creamy, but the grains still firm. (This should take 15–20 minutes depending upon the type of rice used— check the package instructions.) Taste and season with salt and pepper.

Finally, stir in the remaining broth and seafood and let stand with the lid on for 5 minutes. Transfer to a large warmed bowl and sprinkle with parsley. Serve immediately.

My favorite cultivated mushrooms are the large, flat, open, almost black portobellos. They have much more flavor than younger ones with closed caps, and are the next best thing to wild mushrooms. They absorb a lot of butter and I like to get them really brown to concentrate the flavor. Tarragon goes really well with this combination, but don't use too much.

chicken and mushroom risotto *with tarragon*

8 oz. large portobello mushrooms

1 stick plus 3 tablespoons unsalted butter

1 garlic clove, finely chopped

about 6 cups hot chicken broth

1 onion, finely chopped

1 celery stalk, finely chopped

1 1/4 lb. boneless, skinless chicken thighs and breast, finely chopped

2 1/3 cups risotto rice

1 1/4 cups dry white wine

2 teaspoons chopped fresh tarragon

3/4 cup freshly grated Parmesan cheese

sea salt and freshly ground black pepper

chopped fresh parsley, to serve

serves 6

To prepare the mushrooms, cut them into long slices. Melt about half of the butter in a skillet, add the mushrooms and garlic, and sauté over medium heat until browning at the edges. Transfer to a plate and set aside.

Put the broth in a saucepan and keep at a gentle simmer. Melt 2 tablespoons of the remaining butter in a large, heavy saucepan and add the onion and celery. Cook gently for 10 minutes until soft and translucent but not browned. Add the chicken and cook for another 5 minutes, but do not let it color and harden. Stir in the rice until well coated with butter, heated through, and beginning to smell "toasted." Pour in the wine, bring to a boil, and boil hard to reduce by half—this will concentrate the flavor and remove the taste of raw alcohol.

Begin adding the broth, a large ladle at a time, stirring gently until each ladle has been almost absorbed by the rice. The risotto should be kept at a bare simmer throughout cooking, so don't let the rice dry out—add more broth as necessary. Continue until the rice is tender and creamy, but the grains still firm. (This should take 15–20 minutes depending upon the type of rice used—check the package instructions.)

Taste and season well with salt and pepper, then stir in the remaining butter, the tarragon, and Parmesan. Cover and let rest for a couple of minutes. Reheat the mushrooms, then serve the risotto with the mushrooms piled on top, sprinkled with chopped parsley.

ham and leek risotto

The leek is one of my favorite vegetables—it's not used enough.
Its sweet, delicate, onion flavor is an excellent complement to
salty cooked ham. Try to find ham sold in a piece so you can tear
it into shreds—it will be more succulent than sliced ham. Roasting
garlic softens and mellows the flavor until it is almost nutty.

Peel the garlic cloves and put them in a small saucepan. Cover
with olive oil and heat to simmering. Simmer for about 20 minutes
or until the garlic is golden and soft. Let cool in the oil.

Cut the 2 leeks into 3-inch lengths, then slice in half lengthwise
and cut into long, thin shreds. Fill a wok or large saucepan one-
third full with the safflower oil and heat to 375°F, add the
shredded leeks, and deep-fry for 1 minute until crisp and just
golden. Lift out of the oil, drain on paper towels, and set aside.

Slice the remaining leeks (thinly or thickly, as you like) into rings.
Put the broth in a saucepan and keep at a gentle simmer. Heat
⅓ cup of the garlic-flavored olive oil in a large, heavy saucepan.
Add the leeks and sauté for a few minutes until beginning to
soften and color slightly, then stir in the garlic cloves. Pour in the
rice and stir until well coated with oil and heated through.

Begin adding the simmering broth, a large ladle at a time, stirring
gently until each ladle has been almost absorbed by the rice. The
risotto should be kept at a bare simmer throughout cooking, so
don't let the rice dry out—add more broth as necessary. Continue
until the rice is tender and creamy, but the grains still firm. (This
should take 15–20 minutes depending upon the type of rice
used—check the package instructions.) Stir in the mustard and
ham, then season well with salt and pepper. Stir in the Parmesan,
then cover and let rest for a couple of minutes. Serve immediately
topped with a mound of fried leeks.

6 large garlic cloves

about ¾ cup olive oil

1 lb. leeks, plus 2 extra to serve

about 6 cups hot chicken broth

2⅓ cups risotto rice

1 tablespoon grainy mustard

12 oz. cold ham, shredded,
2–2½ cups

½ cup freshly grated
Parmesan cheese

sea salt and freshly ground
black pepper

safflower oil, for deep-frying

serves 4–6

pasta and polenta

There are many variations of this pasta dish in Sicily. The tomato sauce is very rich, but this is balanced by grated *ricotta salata*–ewe's milk ricotta cheese, salted and aged. It is very dry and concentrated, but sharp and salty. The nearest thing you can find to it outside the area is aged pecorino Romano or even feta cheese.

spaghetti *with eggplant and tomato sauce*

3 medium eggplant

1 lb. very ripe red tomatoes (add 2 tablespoons tomato paste if not red enough)

3 tablespoons olive oil

3 garlic cloves, chopped

12 oz. spaghetti or spaghettini

3 tablespoons chopped fresh basil leaves

3–4 tablespoons freshly grated *ricotta salata*, aged pecorino Romano, or Parmesan cheese, plus extra to serve

vegetable oil, for cooking

sea salt

serves 4

Cut the eggplant into small cubes and put in a colander. Sprinkle with salt and put the colander on a plate. Set aside to drain for 30 minutes.

Meanwhile, dip the tomatoes in boiling water for 10 seconds, then drop them into cold water. Slip off the skins, cut in half, and squeeze out and discard the seeds. Chop the flesh coarsely.

Heat the olive oil in a skillet, add the garlic, and sauté for 2–3 minutes until golden. Add the tomatoes and cook for about 15 minutes until the tomatoes begin to disintegrate.

Bring a large saucepan of salted water to a boil, add the spaghetti or spaghettini, and cook according to the package instructions, about 8 minutes.

Meanwhile, rinse the eggplant, drain, and pat dry. Heat about 1 inch vegetable oil in a skillet, add the cubes of eggplant, and sauté until deep golden brown. Remove and drain on paper towels. Stir into the tomato sauce.

Drain the pasta, reserving 2 tablespoons of the cooking water in the pan. Return the pasta to the hot pan. Stir in the tomato and eggplant sauce, basil, and grated cheese. Serve immediately with more cheese sprinkled on top.

Taleggio is a soft cheese and not easy to slice thinly. It is a good idea to freeze the cheese for 10–15 minutes before slicing. Truffle oil has an earthy, intense flavor that goes beautifully with mushrooms—if you have some, add a couple of drops to the cooked mezzalune.

mushroom mezzalune

2 tablespoons olive oil, plus extra to serve

1 garlic clove, finely chopped

8 oz. small cremini mushrooms, sliced

2 tablespoons Marsala wine or medium sherry

1 quantity Fresh Egg Pasta, rolled (page 232)

8 oz. Taleggio cheese, thinly sliced

6 slices of prosciutto, cut in half

sea salt and freshly ground black pepper

to serve

olive oil or truffle oil

fresh basil leaves

a round bowl, about 6 inches diameter

serves 4

Heat the oil in a skillet, add the garlic, and cook for 1 minute. Add the mushrooms, and salt and pepper to taste, and cook for 3–4 minutes until golden. Add the Marsala or sherry, remove from the heat, and let cool.

Put a rolled pasta sheet onto a lightly floured surface. Put the bowl, upside down, on top of the pasta and cut around it with a knife. Repeat to make 12 circles. Put a slice of Taleggio on one side of each circle, spoon the mushrooms on top, and finish with a piece of prosciutto, folded to fit if necessary. Dampen the edges lightly with water and fold each circle over to form a semi-circle, pressing the edges together firmly to enclose the filling and seal.

Bring a large saucepan of water to a boil. Add a good pinch of salt, then half the mezzalune. Cook for 3–4 minutes until they rise to the surface and are cooked through. Drain carefully and keep them warm while you cook the remaining mezzalune. Divide between 4 bowls or plates, sprinkle with olive or truffle oil, and basil leaves, then serve.

Note If you are not cooking the mezzalune immediately, put them in a single layer on a tray lined with nonstick parchment paper, cover with another sheet of parchment paper, and chill for up to 2 hours.

cannelloni *with ricotta, bitter greens, and cherry tomato sauce*

12 dried cannelloni tubes,
12 sheets fresh or dried lasagne,
or 1 recipe Fresh Egg Pasta
(page 232)

tomato sauce

3 tablespoons olive oil

2 garlic cloves, finely chopped

1½ lb. cherry tomatoes,
cut in half

3 tablespoons chopped fresh
basil leaves

sea salt and freshly ground
black pepper

ricotta filling

3 oz. bitter salad greens such as
arugula, watercress, or spinach,
about 2 cups

2 cups ricotta cheese, 16 oz.

2 eggs, beaten

1 cup freshly grated
Parmesan cheese

freshly grated nutmeg, to taste

*a pastry bag with a large
round nozzle*

*a shallow ovenproof dish,
buttered*

serves 4–6

This cannelloni combines a creamy sharp ricotta filling, speckled with slightly bitter greens, and a sweet tomato sauce. The contrast between the sauce and filling is amazing.

To make the tomato sauce, heat the oil in a saucepan, add the garlic, and cook until just turning golden. Add the cherry tomato halves. They should hiss as they go in—this will slightly caramelize the juices, and concentrate the flavor. Stir well, then simmer for 10 minutes. Stir in the basil and season with salt and pepper (the sauce should still appear quite lumpy). Set aside.

To make the ricotta filling, plunge the salad greens into a saucepan of boiling water for 1 minute, then drain well, squeezing out any excess moisture. Chop finely. Press the ricotta through a fine-mesh strainer into a bowl. Beat in the eggs, then add the chopped greens and half the Parmesan. Season with nutmeg, salt, and pepper. Set aside.

Cook the cannelloni or lasagne sheets in a large saucepan of boiling salted water according to the package instructions. If using homemade pasta, cook for 1 minute. Lift out of the water and drain on a clean, lintfree dishtowel.

Spoon the ricotta filling into a pastry bag fitted with a large round nozzle. Fill each tube of cannelloni, or pipe down the shorter edge of each lasagne sheet and roll it up. Arrange the filled pasta tightly together in a single layer in the prepared dish. Spoon the tomato sauce over them and sprinkle with the remaining Parmesan.

Bake in a preheated oven at 400°F for 25–30 minutes until bubbling. Serve immediately.

tomato sauce *with double basil*

3 tablespoons olive oil

2 garlic cloves,
finely chopped

1 shallot, finely chopped

1 cup loosely packed
fresh basil leaves

1 lb. ripe tomatoes, coarsely
chopped, or 14½ oz. can
plum tomatoes

a pinch of sugar

12 oz. dried pasta, such as
spaghetti or linguine

sea salt and freshly ground
black pepper

freshly grated Parmesan
cheese, to serve

serves 4

The basil is added in two stages; first for depth of flavor, then at the end for a burst of fresh fragrance—double basil. In summer, use fragrant, ripe tomatoes.

Heat the oil in a saucepan and add the garlic, shallot, and half the basil. Cook for 3–4 minutes until the shallot is golden.

Add the tomatoes and cook, stirring, for 10 minutes, until thickened and pulpy. Add the sugar, ⅓ cup water, and salt and pepper to taste.

Bring to a boil, cover, and simmer very gently for 1 hour until dark red and thickened, with droplets of oil on the surface.

Bring a large saucepan of salted water to a boil. Add the pasta and cook according to the timings on the package, about 8 minutes.

Drain and return the pasta to the hot pan. Tear the remaining basil into the tomato sauce and add the sauce to the pasta. Toss well, then serve topped with Parmesan.

white spaghetti

This is one of those dishes made from what's on hand that is great when you get home late and hungry. Keep a stock of anchovies, olive oil, and spaghetti and you can always make this dish at short notice.

Bring a large saucepan of salted water to a boil. Add the pasta and cook according to the timings on the package, about 8 minutes.

Put the olive oil and garlic into a small saucepan and heat very gently over low heat for 4–5 minutes until the garlic is pale golden but not browned. Remove and discard the garlic.

Add the anchovies and ⅓ cup water to the pan and simmer rapidly, beating with the fork until the anchovies have almost dissolved into the mixture. Add plenty of black pepper and a pinch of salt.

Drain the pasta and return it to the hot pan. Add the anchovy mixture and toss well. Divide between 2 bowls or plates and serve.

6 oz. dried pasta, such as spaghetti

⅓ cup olive oil

4 garlic cloves, cut in half

6 anchovy fillets in oil, drained

sea salt and freshly ground black pepper

serves 2

Puttanesca was famously named in honor of the ladies of the night, although no one seems quite sure why. Maybe it's because the sauce has a wild and fiery character.

pasta *with puttanesca sauce*

2 tablespoons olive oil

1 onion, finely chopped

2 garlic cloves, finely chopped

4 anchovy fillets in oil, drained and coarsely chopped

2 red chiles, finely chopped

4 ripe tomatoes, coarsely chopped

1 tablespoon salted capers, rinsed well and coarsely chopped

⅓ cup red wine

12 oz. dried pasta, such as gemelli or penne (mostaccioli), about 4½ cups

¾ cup small black olives

2 tablespoons chopped fresh flat-leaf parsley

freshly ground black pepper

freshly grated Parmesan cheese, to serve

serves 4

Heat the oil in a saucepan, then add the onion, garlic, anchovies, and chiles. Cook over medium heat for 4–5 minutes until softened and golden. Add the tomatoes and cook for 3–4 minutes, stirring occasionally, until softened.

Add the capers, wine, and black pepper to taste, then cover and simmer for 20 minutes.

Meanwhile, bring a large saucepan of salted water to a boil. Add the pasta and cook according to the timings on the package, about 8 minutes.

Drain well and return the pasta to the hot pan. Add the tomato sauce, olives, and parsley and toss well. Divide between 4 bowls and serve topped with grated Parmesan.

Smoked salmon (lox) adds a lovely delicate flavor to this dish. Add it right at the last moment so it doesn't overcook or break into tiny pieces.

pasta *with creamy smoked salmon sauce*

10 oz. dried pasta, such as fusilli bucati or farfalle, about 4 1/2 cups

1 1/4 cups heavy cream

2 garlic cloves, crushed

8 oz. smoked salmon (lox), cut into 1/2-inch strips, about 1 1/3 cups

1/4 cup freshly grated Parmesan cheese, plus extra to serve

sea salt and freshly ground black pepper

2 tablespoons chopped fresh chives, to serve

serves 4

Bring a large saucepan of salted water to a boil. Add the pasta and cook according to the timings on the package, about 8 minutes.

Meanwhile, put the cream and garlic in a small saucepan. Season with salt and pepper to taste and heat gently until warmed through.

Drain the pasta and return it to the hot pan. Add the cream, smoked salmon, and Parmesan, toss gently, then divide between 4 bowls or plates. Sprinkle with chives and extra Parmesan, and serve.

Long pasta is the choice for seafood dishes around coastal areas of Italy—spaghetti and spaghettini in the south. This is a simple dish made with local ingredients—nothing sophisticated, but so good. This dish is equally good made with small clams, such as cherrystones.

spaghetti *with mussels, tomatoes, and parsley*

2 lb. live mussels or small clams

½ cup olive oil

1¼ cups dry white wine

16 oz. spaghetti or spaghettini

2 garlic cloves, peeled and crushed

14½ oz. can chopped tomatoes

2 tablespoons chopped fresh flat-leaf parsley

sea salt and freshly ground black pepper

serves 4

Put the mussels in a bowl of cold water and rinse several times to remove any grit or sand. Pull off the beards and scrub well, discarding any that are not firmly closed. Drain.

Heat the oil and wine in a large saucepan and add the mussels. Stir over high heat until the mussels open. Remove and discard any that don't open. Lift out the cooked mussels with a slotted spoon and put them in a bowl. Reserve the cooking liquid.

Bring a large saucepan of salted water to a boil. Add the spaghetti and cook according to the package instructions, about 8 minutes.

Meanwhile, add the garlic to the mussel liquid in the pan. Boil fast to concentrate the flavor. Stir in the tomatoes, return to a boil, and boil fast for 3–4 minutes until reduced. Stir in the mussels and half the parsley and heat through. Taste and season well with salt and pepper.

Drain the pasta, reserving 2 tablespoons of the cooking water in the pan. Return the pasta to the hot pan and stir in the sauce. Sprinkle with the remaining parsley and serve.

Note If any of the mussels are open when you buy them, make sure that when you tap each one sharply against the counter it closes—if not, it is dead and should be thrown away. It's a good idea to soak the mussels in cold water overnight to purify them before cleaning them.

9 oz. dried pasta, such as
fusilli or fusilli bucati,
3–3½ cups

1 tablespoon butter

2 plum tomatoes, coarsely
chopped

1 garlic clove, finely
chopped

¼ cup chile vodka

⅔ cup heavy cream

sea salt and freshly ground
black pepper

to serve

a few chives, cut in half

freshly grated Parmesan
cheese

serves 2

If you haven't got chile vodka, add a small, finely chopped chile at the same time as the garlic and use regular vodka.

creamy vodka sauce

Bring a large saucepan of salted water to a boil. Add the spaghetti and cook according to the package instructions, about 8 minutes.

Meanwhile, heat the butter in a small saucepan, add the tomatoes and garlic, and cook for 3 minutes. Add the vodka and boil rapidly for 2 minutes. Reduce the heat and simmer for 2–3 minutes, then stir in the cream and simmer gently for another 5 minutes. Add salt and pepper to taste.

Drain the pasta and return it to the hot pan. Add the creamy sauce to the pasta and mix well. Transfer to 2 serving bowls and top with chives. Sprinkle with plenty of Parmesan and black pepper, and serve.

pasta *with carbonara sauce*

This is traditionally served with spaghetti, but any long or ribbon shape, such as tagliatelle or linguine, will be fine.

Bring a large saucepan of salted water to a boil. Add the spaghetti and cook according to the package instructions, about 8 minutes.

Meanwhile, heat the butter in a small skillet, add the shallot, garlic, and bacon, and cook for 5 minutes until golden. Put the eggs, cream, and Parmesan into a bowl and beat, adding salt and pepper to taste.

Drain the pasta and return it to the hot pan. Remove the pan from the heat and add the shallot mixture. Add the egg mixture and toss well. Divide between 2 serving bowls, sprinkle with Parmesan and black pepper, then serve immediately.

7 oz. dried pasta, such as
spaghetti or linguine

1 tablespoon butter

1 shallot, finely chopped

2 garlic cloves, finely
chopped

6 slices of bacon, chopped

2 eggs

⅔ cup light cream

2 tablespoons freshly
grated Parmesan cheese,
plus extra to serve

sea salt and freshly ground
black pepper

serves 2

about 12 sheets of dried or fresh *lasagne verdi*, made from Spinach Pasta (page 232) rolled out to the second to last setting on the pasta machine

double recipe Béchamel Sauce (page 229)

about 1/2 cup freshly grated Parmesan cheese

ragù

3 oz. pancetta (about 1/2 cup) or dry-cure smoked bacon in a piece

4 oz. chicken livers, about 1/2 cup

4 tablespoons butter

1 medium onion, finely chopped

1 medium carrot, chopped

1 celery stalk, finely chopped

8 oz. lean ground beef, about 1 cup

2 tablespoons tomato paste

1/4 cup dry white wine

3/4 cup beef broth or water

freshly grated nutmeg

sea salt and freshly ground black pepper

a deep baking dish, 10 x 8 inches, buttered

serves 4–6

The classic version of this dish is pasta layered with meat sauce and creamy *salsa besciamella* (béchamel sauce). It is very easy to assemble. Make the *ragù* the day before, and the *besciamella* on the day. If you use fresh pasta, it doesn't need precooking, and is layered up as it is. Just make sure the meat sauce is quite liquid. This will be absorbed into the pasta as it bakes.

lasagne al forno

To make the ragù, cut the pancetta into small cubes. Trim the chicken livers, removing any fat or gristle. Cut off any discolored bits, which will be bitter if left on. Coarsely chop the livers.

Melt the butter in a saucepan, add the pancetta, and cook for 2–3 minutes until beginning to brown. Add the onion, carrot, and celery, and brown these, too. Stir in the ground beef and brown until just changing color, but not hardening—break it up with a wooden spoon. Stir in the chicken livers and cook for 2–3 minutes. Add the tomato paste, mix well, and pour in the wine and broth. Season well with nutmeg, salt, and pepper. Bring to a boil, cover, and simmer very gently for as long as you can—2 hours if possible.

If using dried lasagne, cook the sheets in plenty of boiling water in batches according to the package instructions. Lift out with a slotted spoon and drain on a clean, lintfree dishtowel. Fresh pasta will not need boiling.

Spoon one-third of the meat sauce into a buttered baking dish. Cover with 4 sheets of lasagne and spread with one-third of the béchamel sauce. Repeat twice more, finishing with a layer of béchamel sauce covering the whole top. Sprinkle with Parmesan cheese. Bake in a preheated oven at 350°F for about 45 minutes until brown and bubbling. Let stand for 10 minutes to settle and firm up before serving.

Fontina is one of the oldest cheeses made in the Valle d'Aosta. It is rich and nutty, and melts very easily. It is also the basis of a type of fondue called *fonduta*. This polenta dish is typical fare in some of the little family restaurants you come across off the trail when skiing in Italy. Just the stuff to keep the cold out.

baked polenta *with fontina and pancetta*

If using instant polenta, cook according to the package instructions, then turn out into a mound on a wooden board, then let cool and set.

If using regular polenta (cornmeal), bring 4 cups salted water to a boil, then slowly sprinkle in the cornmeal through your fingers, whisking all the time to stop lumps forming. Cook, stirring with a wooden spoon, for 45 minutes on low heat and then turn out into a mound on a wooden board and let cool and set.

Meanwhile, slice the fontina thinly or grate it. Cut the polenta into slices about ½-inch thick. Arrange a layer of polenta in the ovenproof dish. Top with half the fontina and half the Parmesan. Season with salt and pepper. Add another layer of polenta, then cover with the remaining fontina and Parmesan. Finally, add a layer of pancetta.

Bake in a preheated oven at 350°F for 40 minutes until brown and bubbling and the pancetta crisping on top. Remove from the oven and serve.

2 cups instant polenta or coarsely-ground cornmeal

12 oz. fontina, raclette, or a mixture of grated mozzarella and Cheddar cheese

1 cup freshly grated Parmesan cheese

6 oz. thinly sliced smoked pancetta, about 1 cup

sea salt and freshly ground black pepper

a shallow ovenproof baking dish, 10 x 8 inches, buttered

serves 6

soft polenta *with sausage ragù*

This is a real winter-warmer from the north of Italy where polenta is the staple carbohydrate. I have been to a polenta night where the steaming soft cornmeal was poured straight onto a huge wooden board set in the middle of the table. The sauce was poured into a large hollow in the center of the polenta and everyone gathered round to help themselves directly from the pile—no plates necessary.

2 teaspoons salt

2 cups instant polenta

freshly grated Parmesan cheese, to serve

sausage ragù

1 lb. fresh Italian pork sausages

2 tablespoons olive oil

1 medium onion, finely chopped

2 cups tomato passata (strained crushed tomatoes)

²/₃ cup dry red wine

6 sun-dried tomatoes in oil, drained and sliced

sea salt and freshly ground black pepper

serves 4

To make the ragù, squeeze the sausage meat out of the skins into a bowl and break up the meat. Heat the oil in a medium saucepan and add the onion. Cook for 5 minutes until soft and golden. Stir in the sausage meat, browning it all over and breaking up the lumps with a wooden spoon. Pour in the passata and the wine. Bring to a boil. Add the sun-dried tomatoes. Simmer for 30 minutes or until well reduced, stirring occasionally. Add salt and pepper to taste.

Meanwhile, bring 5½ cups water to a boil with 2 teaspoons salt. Sprinkle in the polenta, stirring or whisking to prevent lumps forming.

Simmer for 5–10 minutes, stirring constantly, until thickened like soft mashed potato. Quickly spoon the polenta into 4 large, warm soup plates and make a hollow in the center of each. Top with the sausage ragù and serve with grated Parmesan cheese.

A warming winter dish to eat by a roaring fire. This is sublime comfort food, loaded with sausage and strings of melting cheese. At the risk of being sacrilegious, Spanish chorizo would be great in this dish. Add chopped herbs to the polenta, if you like, or even a little chopped chile.

polenta baked
with italian sausage and cheese

2 cups instant polenta or coarsely-ground cornmeal

1 lb. fresh Italian pork sausages

1 tablespoon olive oil

1 red onion, finely chopped

²/₃ cup meat or Vegetable Broth (page 234)

3 tablespoons chopped fresh rosemary and sage, mixed

12 oz. Taleggio cheese, chopped or grated, 3¹/₂ cups

1¹/₂ cups freshly grated Parmesan cheese

a few pieces of butter

sea salt and freshly ground black pepper

a shallow ovenproof dish, buttered

serves 6

If using instant polenta, cook according to the package instructions, then turn out into a mound on a wooden board, then let cool and set.

If using regular polenta (cornmeal), bring 4 cups salted water to a boil, then slowly sprinkle in the cornmeal through your fingers, whisking all the time to stop lumps forming. Cook, stirring with a wooden spoon, for 45 minutes on low heat and then turn out into a mound on a wooden board and let cool and set.

Slice the sausages very thickly. Heat the olive oil in a nonstick skillet, add the sausage, and sauté until browned on all sides. Add the onion and cook for 5 minutes until softening. Add the broth and half the chopped herbs, salt, and pepper.

Cut the polenta into ¹/₂-inch slices. Arrange a layer of polenta in the prepared dish. Add half the sausage mixture, half the Taleggio, and half the Parmesan, in layers. Cover with another layer of polenta, add layers of the remaining sausage mixture, Taleggio, and Parmesan, and dot with a few pieces of butter. Sprinkle with the remaining herbs.

Bake in a preheated oven at 350°F for 40 minutes until brown and bubbling.

Soft and golden, these gnocchi are a staple in the Lazio area around Rome. I have added herbs and mustard to the basic mix and like to serve them with roasted rabbit or lamb.

roman gnocchi *with herbs and semolina*

Pour the milk into a saucepan and whisk in the semolina. Bring slowly to a boil, stirring all the time until it really thickens—about 10 minutes (it should be quite thick, like choux paste). Beat in half the Parmesan, half the butter, the egg yolks, mustard, sage, and parsley. Add salt and pepper to taste.

Spread the gnocchi mixture onto the lined baking sheet to a depth of ½ inch. Let cool and set, about 2 hours.

When set, cut the gnocchi into triangles or circles with the cookie cutter. Spread the trimmings from the chopped gnocchi in the bottom of the ovenproof dish. Dot with some of the remaining butter and sprinkle with a little Parmesan. Arrange the gnocchi triangles or circles in a single layer over the trimmings. Dot with the remaining butter and Parmesan. Bake in a preheated oven at 400°F for 20–25 minutes until golden and crusty. Let stand for 5 minutes, then serve.

1 quart milk

1²/₃ cups semolina

1³/₄ cups freshly grated Parmesan cheese

1 stick butter

2 egg yolks

1 tablespoon Dijon mustard

2 tablespoons chopped fresh sage leaves

3 tablespoons chopped fresh flat-leaf parsley

sea salt and freshly ground black pepper

a baking tray lined with plastic wrap

a cookie cutter, 2 inches diameter

an ovenproof dish, 10 x 8 inches, well buttered

serves 4–6

pizzas, tarts, and bread

The secret to a delicious Marinara is in the tomatoes. Choose really ripe, plump varieties. It's well worth the extra effort of peeling and seeding them—the result is a satin-smooth, fragrant, and fruity sauce. Don't be tempted to add any cheese.

marinara pizza

Put a pizza stone or baking tray in the oven and preheat the oven to 425°F.

Meanwhile, dip the tomatoes in boiling water for 10 seconds, then drop them into cold water. Slip off and discard the skins, cut the tomatoes in half, and squeeze out and discard the seeds. Chop the flesh coarsely.

Heat 2 tablespoons of the oil in a saucepan, then add the tomatoes and salt and pepper to taste. Cook for about 5 minutes, stirring occasionally, until thickened.

Roll out the dough on a lightly floured counter to a circle 12 inches diameter and brush with a little oil. Spoon the tomato sauce over the top and sprinkle evenly with the garlic and oregano or marjoram. Sprinkle with a little more oil.

Carefully transfer the pizza to the hot pizza stone or baking tray and cook in the preheated oven for 15–20 minutes, until crisp and golden. Serve immediately.

about 1 1/2 lb. ripe tomatoes

3–4 tablespoons olive oil

1 recipe Basic Pizza Dough (page 231)

3 garlic cloves, very thinly sliced

1 tablespoon chopped fresh oregano or marjoram

sea salt and freshly ground black pepper

a pizza stone or baking tray

serves 2

The recipe for this pizza dough was given to me by a gravel-voiced *pizzaiolo* in Sicily. He insists that using a touch of lemon juice in the dough makes it light and crisp, and I have to agree. Use ordinary all-purpose flour, if you prefer.

margherita pizza

1²/₃ cups fine Italian semolina flour (*farina di semola*)

½ cake compressed fresh yeast

1 tablespoon lemon juice

1 tablespoon olive oil, plus extra for trickling

a pinch of salt

about 1¼ cups warm water

pizza topping

1 recipe Pizza Maker's Tomato Sauce (page 228)

8 oz. fresh mozzarella cheese, thinly sliced

a good handful of fresh basil leaves

sea salt and freshly ground black pepper

2 pizza stones or baking trays

2 baking trays lined with nonstick baking parchment

serves 4

To make the dough, put the semolina flour in a bowl, crumble the fresh yeast into the flour, add the lemon juice, olive oil, and a generous pinch of salt, then add enough of the warm water to form a very soft dough. Transfer to a floured counter and knead for 10 minutes or until smooth and elastic. Put the dough in a clean, oiled bowl (or an oiled plastic bag), cover, and let rise until doubled in size (about 1 hour).

Put the pizza stone or baking trays in the oven and preheat the oven to 425°F.

Cut the dough in half and knead each half into a round. Pat or roll the rounds into 10-inch circles, keeping the bottoms well floured. Transfer the pizzas onto baking trays lined with nonstick parchment paper. Spread each one lightly with tomato sauce, cover with sliced mozzarella, and season with salt and pepper. Let rise in a warm place for 10 minutes, then open the oven door, and slide paper and pizza onto the hot pizza stones or baking trays.

Bake in the preheated oven for 18–20 minutes, until the crust is golden and the cheese melted but still white. Remove from the oven, sprinkle with basil leaves and olive oil, then eat immediately.

Note Semolina flour is very finely ground and needs no extra flour. You can grind ordinary semolina into fine flour by working it in a blender for about 2 minutes.

roasted bell pepper pizza

Roasting bell peppers brings out their sweetness. Make sure they are still warm when you add them to the dressing, so that they absorb the flavors of the garlic and parsley.

Put a pizza stone or baking tray in the oven and preheat to 425°F. Put the peppers in a small roasting pan and bake for 30 minutes in the hot oven, turning them occasionally, until the skin blisters and blackens.

Meanwhile, put the garlic and parsley in a bowl. Add the oil, and salt and pepper to taste.

Remove the peppers from the oven, cover with a clean, lintfree dishcloth, and set aside for about 10 minutes, until cool enough to handle but still warm. Pierce the bottom of each pepper and squeeze the juices into the parsley and oil mixture. Peel and seed the peppers. Cut the flesh into 1-inch strips and add to the mixture in the bowl. Mix briefly, cover, and set aside at room temperature until needed.

Roll out the dough on a lightly floured counter to a circle 12 inches diameter and brush with a little oil. Spoon the tomato sauce over the dough and arrange the tomatoes and mozzarella on top. Spoon the pepper mixture over the top.

Carefully transfer to the hot pizza stone or baking tray and cook in the preheated oven for 20–25 minutes, until crisp and golden. Serve immediately.

2 red bell peppers

2 yellow bell peppers

2 garlic cloves, finely chopped

a small bunch of fresh flat-leaf parsley, finely chopped

2 tablespoons olive oil

1 recipe Basic Pizza Dough (page 231)

1 recipe Pizza Maker's Tomato Sauce (page 228)

2 tomatoes, sliced or cut in half, about 2 cups

6 oz. mozzarella cheese, drained and sliced, about 1½ cups

sea salt and freshly ground black pepper

a pizza stone or baking tray

serves 2

Mushrooms are always an excellent choice for pizza toppings. For a range of flavors and textures, use a mixture of varieties, including cremini, shiitake, and button mushrooms. The basil, chile, and garlic oil isn't essential, but adds a kick.

mushroom pizza *with basil, chiles, and garlic oil*

1 recipe Basic Pizza Dough (page 231)

½ cup olive oil

1 recipe Pizza Maker's Tomato Sauce (page 228)

2½ cups thickly sliced mixed mushrooms

6 oz. mozzarella cheese, drained and chopped, about 1½ cups

2 plump garlic cloves, cut in half

1 large, mild red chile, seeded and quartered

8 fresh basil leaves, finely shredded

sea salt and freshly ground black pepper

a pizza stone or baking tray

serves 2

Put a pizza stone or baking tray in the oven and preheat the oven to 425°F.

Roll out the dough on a lightly floured counter to a circle 12 inches diameter and brush with a little oil. Spoon the tomato sauce on top and sprinkle with the mushrooms and mozzarella.

Sprinkle the pizza with a little oil and season with salt and pepper. Carefully transfer to the hot pizza stone or baking tray and cook in the preheated oven for 20–25 minutes, until crisp and golden.

Meanwhile, put the remaining oil in a small saucepan with the garlic and chile. Heat very gently for 10 minutes, until the garlic is softened and translucent. Remove from the heat and set aside to cool slightly for 5 minutes.

Using a fork, remove and discard the garlic and chile. Stir the basil into the flavored oil and sprinkle over the hot pizza. Serve immediately.

Bresaola, dried lean beef from the Alpine region of Italy, has a lovely sweetness which here complements the peppery arugula and salty Parmesan. If you can't find bresaola, use a dry-cure ham, such as prosciutto.

eggplant pizza *with bresaola, arugula, and parmesan*

1 eggplant, cut into ½-inch slices

¼ cup olive oil, plus extra to serve

1 recipe Basic Pizza Dough (page 231)

1 recipe Pizza Maker's Tomato Sauce (page 228)

4 oz. very thinly sliced bresaola or cured ham, about 1 cup

1½ cups arugula leaves, torn

Parmesan cheese shavings

sea salt and freshly ground black pepper

a pizza stone or baking tray

serves 2

Put a pizza stone or baking tray in the oven and preheat the oven to 400°F.

Brush the eggplant slices with the oil and sprinkle salt and pepper lightly on both sides. Preheat a stovetop grill pan, lay the eggplant slices on it, and cook for 3–4 minutes on each side, until tender and browned.

Roll out the dough on a lightly floured counter to a circle 12 inches diameter and brush with a little oil. Spoon the tomato sauce onto the pizza and arrange the eggplant slices on top.

Transfer to the hot pizza stone or baking tray and cook in the preheated oven for 15 minutes. Remove from the oven and scatter the bresaola or ham evenly across the pizza. Return the pizza to the oven and cook for another 5–10 minutes, until crisp and golden.

Sprinkle with the arugula and Parmesan. Top with a splash of olive oil and a good grinding of black pepper. Serve immediately.

quattro stagioni pizza

The pizza for people who just can't make up
their minds which one they want. You get all
your favorites at once with this recipe.

¼ cup olive oil

1 shallot, thinly sliced

1 cup cremini mushrooms, sliced
(if unavailable, use white mushrooms)

2 tablespoons chopped fresh parsley

1 recipe Basic Pizza Dough (page 231)

1 recipe Pizza Maker's Tomato Sauce
(page 228)

2 oz. prosciutto, shredded, about ¾ cup

6 black olives

4 artichoke hearts in brine or oil,
drained and quartered

3 oz. mozzarella cheese, drained

4 anchovy fillets in oil, drained

sea salt and freshly ground black pepper

fresh basil leaves, to serve

a pizza stone or baking tray

serves 2

Put a pizza stone or baking tray in the oven and preheat the oven to 400°F.

Heat 2 tablespoons of the oil in a skillet, add the shallot, and cook for 2 minutes. Add the mushrooms and cook for another 2–3 minutes, until softened and golden. Stir in the parsley and add salt and pepper to taste.

Roll out the dough on a lightly floured counter to a circle 12 inches diameter and brush with a little oil. Spoon the tomato sauce over the top.

Pile the mushrooms over one-quarter of the pizza. Arrange the ham and olives on another quarter and the artichoke hearts on the third section of pizza. Slice the mozzarella and arrange it on the remaining section and put the anchovies on top. Sprinkle a little more oil over the whole pizza, then add salt and pepper.

Carefully transfer to the hot pizza stone or baking tray and cook in the preheated oven for 20–25 minutes, until crisp and golden. Cut into quarters, sprinkle the basil over the artichoke portion, and serve immediately.

In general, Italians like to stick to the classics when it comes to pizza, but as you can see below, pizza toppings are limitless. I have taken inspiration from a dish I had in Verona, and applied it to a pizza—well, it's just bread and cheese after all, isn't it?

potato pizza

½ oz. compressed fresh yeast or 1 tablespoon active dry yeast

a pinch of sugar

1 cup warm water

2⅓ cups all-purpose flour plus extra, for dusting

1 tablespoon olive oil, plus extra for trickling

a pinch of salt

potato topping

1 medium potato, peeled and very thinly sliced

6 oz. fontina, Taleggio, or mozzarella cheese, about 1½ cups

1 large head of radicchio, cut into about 8 wedges, brushed with olive oil and grilled or broiled for 5 minutes

1 tablespoon chopped fresh thyme

sea salt and freshly ground black pepper

a baking pan, about 11 x 13 inches

serves 2–4

To make the dough, put the fresh yeast and sugar in a medium bowl and beat until creamy. Whisk in the warm water and leave for 10 minutes until frothy. For other yeasts, use according to the package instructions.

Sift the flour into a large bowl and make a hollow in the center. Pour in the yeast mixture, olive oil, and a good pinch of salt. Mix with a round-bladed knife, then your hands, until the dough comes together. Transfer to a floured counter, wash and dry your hands, and knead for 10 minutes until smooth and elastic. The dough should be quite soft, but if too soft to handle, add more flour, 1 tablespoon at a time. Put the dough in a clean, oiled bowl, cover with a damp, lintfree dishtowel or plastic wrap, and let rise until doubled in size—about 1 hour.

When risen, punch down the dough with your fists, then roll out or pat into a rectangle that will fit in the baking pan, pushing it up the sides a little. Cover the top with a thin layer of sliced potato, then half the cheese, the wedges of radicchio, then the remaining cheese. Season with salt and pepper, and sprinkle with thyme.

Trickle oil over the top and let rise in a warm place for 10 minutes. Bake in a preheated oven at 425°F for 15–20 minutes or until golden and bubbling.

I will never forget this tart. I ate it way down in the toe of Italy on my way to Sicily. The tart was turned out before us on the little table—the tomatoes could not have been more red nor the basil more green.

tomato upside-down tart *with basil*

Cut the tomatoes in half across their middle. Arrange, cut side up, in the shallow tart pan so that they fit tightly together. Mix the garlic and oregano with the olive oil, salt, and pepper. Spoon or brush the mixture over the cut tomatoes.

Bake in a preheated oven at 325°F for about 2 hours, checking from time to time. They should be slightly shrunk and still brilliantly red. If too dark, they will be bitter. Let cool in the pan (if the pan is very burned, remove the tomatoes, wash the pan, brush it with oil, and return the tomatoes to it). Increase the oven temperature to 400°F.

Roll out the dough to a circle slightly bigger than the pan. Using the rolling pin to help you, lift up the dough and unroll it over the pan, letting the edges drape over the sides. Lightly press the dough down over the tomatoes, but do not trim the edges yet. Bake for 20 minutes until golden.

Let settle for 5 minutes, then trim off the overhanging edges and invert onto a plate. Sprinkle with olive oil and basil leaves and serve.

8–10 large ripe plum tomatoes (size depending upon what will fit the pan)

2 garlic cloves, finely chopped

1 tablespoon dried oregano

¼ cup extra virgin olive oil, plus extra to serve

8 oz. puff pastry dough

sea salt and freshly ground black pepper

a good handful of fresh basil leaves, to serve

a shallow tart pan or sauté pan, 9 inches diameter

serves 4

Focaccia literally means "a bread that was baked on the hearth," but it is easy to bake in conventional ovens. I make this one in a pan, but it can be shaped on a baking tray to any shape you want. Although a rustic focaccia can be made with any basic pizza dough, the secret of a truly light focaccia lies in three risings, and dimpling the dough with your fingers so it traps olive oil while it bakes.

focaccia al rosmarino

5 cups Italian-style flour or all-purpose flour, plus extra for kneading

¹/₂ teaspoon fine salt

1¹/₂ cakes compressed fresh yeast (for active dry yeast, use 1¹/₂ packages and follow the package instructions)

²/₃ cup good olive oil

2 cups warm water

coarse sea salt

sprigs of rosemary

a water spray

2 shallow cake pans, or pie or pizza plates, 10 inches diameter, lightly oiled

makes 2 thick focacce, 10 inches diameter

Sift the flour and fine salt into a large bowl and make a hollow in the center. Crumble in the yeast. Pour in 3 tablespoons of the olive oil, then rub in the yeast until the mixture resembles fine bread crumbs. Pour in the warm water and mix with your hands until the dough comes together.

Transfer the dough to a floured counter, wash and dry your hands, and knead for 10 minutes until smooth and elastic. The dough should be quite soft, but if too soft to handle, knead in more flour, 1 tablespoon at a time. Put the dough in a clean oiled bowl, cover with a damp, lintfree dishtowel or plastic wrap, and let rise in a warm place until doubled in size, 30–90 minutes.

Punch down the dough and cut in half. Put on a floured counter and shape each half into a round ball. Roll out into 2 circles, 10 inches diameter, and put in the pans. Cover with a damp, lintfree dishtowel or plastic wrap and let rise for 30 minutes.

Remove the dishtowel and, using your finger tips, make dimples all over the surface of the dough. They can be quite deep. Pour over the remaining oil and sprinkle generously with coarse salt. Cover again and let rise for 30 minutes. Spray with water, sprinkle the rosemary on top, and bake in a preheated oven at 400°F for 20–25 minutes. Transfer to a wire rack to cool. Eat the same day or freeze immediately. Serve with a meal, or as a snack with oil and vinegar for dipping and olives.

rosemary and onion schiacciata

Schiacciata is the Tuscan word for flat bread, usually baked on the hearth. It is the ancestor of modern pizza.

To make the pizza dough, beat the fresh yeast and sugar in a small bowl, then beat in the warm water. Leave for 10 minutes until frothy. For other yeasts, use according to the package instructions.

Sift the flour into a large bowl and make a well in the center. Pour in the yeast mixture, olive oil, salt, and rosemary. Mix with a round-bladed knife, then bring the dough together with your hands. Transfer to a floured counter. With clean dry hands, knead the dough for 10 minutes until smooth, elastic, and quite soft. (If too soft to handle, knead in a little more flour.) Place in a clean oiled bowl, cover with a damp, lintfree dishtowel, and let rise for about 1 hour or until doubled in size.

Finely slice the onions. Heat the oil in a heavy saucepan. Add the onions and cook over gentle heat, stirring occasionally, for 40 minutes to 1 hour until they are completely soft and golden—they must not brown. Stir in the chopped rosemary.

Preheat the oven to 450°F. Punch down the dough with your hands and roll out, or stretch with your fingers, to a rectangle or 12-inch circle on the baking tray. Spoon the onions on top of the pizza and spread them evenly. Dot with the mozzarella, anchovies, and olives. Sprinkle with olive oil.

Bake in the preheated oven for 15–20 minutes until golden and crisp. Top with rosemary leaves and serve immediately.

1 cake compressed fresh yeast, or 1 package active dry yeast

a pinch of sugar

1 cup warm water

2$\frac{1}{3}$ cups all-purpose flour

2 tablespoons olive oil

$\frac{1}{2}$ teaspoon salt

1 tablespoon chopped fresh rosemary

onion topping

6–8 medium onions, about 2 lb.

3 tablespoons olive oil, plus extra for sprinkling

1 tablespoon chopped fresh rosemary

6 oz. mozzarella, thinly sliced, about 1$\frac{1}{2}$ cups

12 anchovies in oil, drained

16 black olives, such as Niçoise, pitted

sprigs of rosemary, to serve

a large baking tray, floured

serves 4

salads, vegetables, and legumes

2–3 medium salad potatoes,
about 12 oz., peeled

6 oz. fine green beans, trimmed,
about 1 ¼ cups

extra virgin olive oil

¼ cup black or green
olives, pitted

1 small crisp lettuce

2 large ripe tomatoes, peeled
and quartered (or unripe
to be authentic)

3 tablespoons chopped
fresh flat-leaf parsley

sea salt and freshly ground
black pepper

to serve

a small bottle of good olive oil

a small bottle of red wine vinegar

serves 4

If you ask for a mixed salad in Italy, this is what you will get. Don't be surprised if the tomatoes are not red ripe, but hard and green—this is how they are eaten in salads. This dish is to cleanse the palate after a meat or fish course, and that is just what it does. Leaving the skins on potatoes and tomatoes is generally not done, but you can if you prefer.

italian mixed salad

Boil the potatoes in salted water for about 15 minutes or until tender, adding the beans 4 minutes before the potatoes are ready. Drain, then cover with cold water to stop the cooking.

When cold, drain well. Remove the beans to a bowl, slice the potatoes thickly, and add to the beans, moistening with a little olive oil. Add the olives and toss well.

Wash the lettuce and tear into bite-size pieces. Add the lettuce and tomatoes to the potatoes and beans and toss lightly. Transfer to a serving bowl and sprinkle with parsley, salt, and pepper. Serve the olive oil and vinegar separately and dress the salad at the table.

In Sicily, the land of orange and lemon groves, this salad is often served after grilled fish—especially in the region around Palermo. It is another example of their passion for sweet and savory combinations and is very refreshing.

orange, frisée, and black olive salad

2 oranges

1 red onion

4 oz. frisée or escarole, about 2 cups

dressing

finely grated zest and juice of 1 unwaxed orange

⅓ cup extra virgin olive oil

2 tablespoons thinly sliced fresh basil leaves

2 tablespoons finely chopped, pitted, Greek-style, oven-dried black olives

2 sun-dried tomatoes in oil, finely chopped

sea salt and freshly ground black pepper

serves 4

To make the dressing, put the orange zest and juice, olive oil, basil, olives, and sun-dried tomatoes in a large bowl. Mix well, season with salt and pepper, and set aside to develop the flavors.

Peel the oranges with a sharp knife, removing all the skin and white pith. Divide into segments. Thinly slice the onion, using a very sharp, thin-bladed knife or a Japanese mandoline. Immediately toss the onion and oranges in the dressing to prevent discoloration. Let marinate in a cool place for 15 minutes.

Put the frisée on a plate and pile the dressed orange and onion mixture in the center, spooning any remaining dressing over the top. Serve immediately.

beet, wheat, and arugula salad

Farro is an ancient form of wheat that is often used in Italy to make soups, salads, and even desserts. You can find it in gourmet stores, or under the name "wheat berries" or "wheat grains" in health food stores. It is delicious and chewy and makes a wonderful earthy salad combined with sweet beets and warm dressing. Barley makes a good substitute. Serve this salad warm.

Drain the soaked farro and put in a large saucepan with the onion, carrot, celery, bay leaf, and crushed garlic cloves. Add water to cover. Bring to a boil, turn down the heat, and simmer for about 45 minutes or until tender and firm but not falling apart and mushy. Drain, then remove and discard the vegetables.

Heat 2 tablespoons of the olive oil in a skillet and cook the pancetta until golden and crisp. Remove the pancetta and drain on paper towels. Return the pan to the heat and add the beets. Sauté for 2–3 minutes, then add to the bowl of pancetta.

Add the chopped garlic to the hot pan and sauté until just browning. Immediately deglaze the pan with the red wine vinegar and add the sugar, boiling until it has dissolved. Pour in the remaining olive oil, stir well, and heat gently but do not boil. Add salt and pepper to taste. Put the farro, pancetta, beets, scallions, and arugula in a large bowl and mix gently. Pour in the dressing and toss lightly but thoroughly. Serve immediately before it becomes soggy.

1½ cups *farro* (or wheat berries), soaked in cold water for 2 hours

1 small onion, cut in half

1 carrot, peeled and cut in half

1 celery stalk, cut in half

1 bay leaf

2 whole garlic cloves, lightly crushed but kept whole

⅔ cup extra virgin olive oil

4 oz. pancetta (Italian bacon), cut into matchsticks, about 1 cup

1 lb. small cooked beets, peeled and quartered

1 fat garlic clove, finely chopped

3 tablespoons red wine vinegar

½ teaspoon sugar

6 scallions, white and green parts chopped

a large bunch of arugula, about 10 oz., torn if the leaves are large

sea salt and freshly ground black pepper

serves 4

In Sicily, onions are roasted in huge metal trays, then put on display outside vegetable stores. Sicilians love the sweetness of onions cooked like this. Normally the onions are simply squeezed out of their skins after roasting. However, I think they taste even better finished off with a sweet and sour sauce.

whole onions baked in their skins

Trim the root end of each onion so that they will stand up securely. Rub with olive oil. Cut a deep cross in the top of each one, slicing towards the base so that it is cut almost into quarters.

Pack closely together in a flameproof roasting pan. Sprinkle with oil, salt, and pepper. Bake in a preheated oven at 375°F for 1 to 1¼ hours, until tender in the center.

Lift out the onions onto a serving dish, leaving the juices behind. Set the roasting pan over medium heat and add the wine, vinegar, raisins, fennel seeds, and capers. Scrape up any sediment and boil for a couple of minutes until reduced and syrupy.

Taste, add salt and pepper if necessary, then pour the sauce over the onions and sprinkle with chopped fresh parsley.

6 large white, red, or yellow onions

olive oil, for basting and serving

⅔ cup white wine

3 tablespoons red wine vinegar

2 tablespoons golden raisins

1 teaspoon fennel seeds

1 tablespoon small salted capers, rinsed

sea salt and freshly ground black pepper

2–3 tablespoons chopped fresh flat-leaf parsley, to serve

a flameproof roasting pan

serves 6

sicilian green vegetables

This is traditionally cooked for quite some time (about
45 minutes), because it used to be made with dried beans, but
I have shortened the cooking time to keep the freshness and
color of the vegetables. It is often served as a soup, or you can
add creamy ricotta to make a light lunch.

2 cups shelled fava beans,
fresh or frozen and thawed,
(1¾ lb. before shelling)

¼ cup olive oil

8 oz. scallions, coarsely chopped,
about 2 cups

4 fresh, canned, or frozen
artichoke hearts, quartered

1¼ cups Vegetable Broth
(page 234) or water

2 cups shelled peas,
fresh or frozen and thawed
(1 lb. before shelling)

a good pinch of sugar, to taste

2 tablespoons chopped fresh
mint leaves

sea salt and freshly ground
black pepper

serves 4

If using fresh artichokes, see the note on page 32 for how to prepare them. Drain them just before using.

Bring a large saucepan of salted water to a boil, add the fava beans, and boil for 1 minute. Drain and plunge them into a bowl of cold water to cool them quickly and set the color. Nick the bean's pale outer skin at the top of the bean and gently squeeze at the bottom to pop the bright green bean out. Continue until all are done.

Heat the oil, add the scallions, and cook over gentle heat for a couple of minutes until they wilt and soften, but do not let brown. Add the fresh artichokes, if using, then the broth or water. Season well with salt and pepper, bring to a boil, then reduce the heat and simmer for 5 minutes.

Add the peas and cook for another 5 minutes, then gently stir in the fava beans and canned or defrosted artichoke hearts, if using. Simmer for another 3–4 minutes. Remove from the heat, taste, add a good pinch of sugar, then stir in the mint. Let cool so the flavors will develop. Serve at room temperature.

Fresh young artichokes are wonderful cooked in this simple way. They are easy to prepare, but it is worth wearing light rubber gloves to prevent black fingers. Baby artichokes are quite different from the fat, globe ones. They are slightly smaller than your hand, elongated, purple-green, and usually sold in bunches.

sautéed artichokes

with thyme and cool ricotta

8–12 medium purple-green artichokes with stems and heads, about 4 inches long

1½ lemons

½ cup good olive oil

1–2 tablespoons chopped fresh thyme

⅔ cup dry white wine

at least 4 oz. fresh ricotta cheese, about 1 cup

sea salt and freshly ground black pepper

serves 4

To prepare the artichokes, see the note on page 32. When ready to cook them, drain and cut them in half lengthwise.

Heat the olive oil in a large skillet until hot, then add the artichokes. Sauté for 3 minutes without moving them, then turn them over and cook for another 2–3 minutes until tender. Transfer to a warm serving dish.

Add the thyme to the pan and cook over high heat for a few seconds to release the aroma. Add the wine and boil hard to reduce by half. Season with a squeeze of lemon juice, salt, and pepper. Crumble the ricotta around the edge of the plate of artichokes and pour the hot thyme sauce on top. Serve immediately.

These firm but juicy tomatoes burst with the flavor of the sun. They take no time to prepare, but need a long time in the oven and smell fantastic while cooking. Plum tomatoes have less moisture and work well, but you can use any vine-ripened variety, just as long as they have some taste.

slow-roasted tomatoes
with garlic and oregano

6–10 ripe plum tomatoes

2 garlic cloves, finely chopped

1 tablespoon dried oregano

¼ cup extra virgin olive oil

sea salt and freshly ground black pepper

fresh basil leaves, to serve

a baking tray

serves 4

Cut the tomatoes in half lengthwise (or horizontally if using round tomatoes). Put them, cut side up, on the baking tray.

Put the garlic, oregano, olive oil, salt, and pepper in a bowl and mix well, then spoon or brush the mixture over the cut tomatoes.

Bake in a preheated oven at 325°F for 1½–2 hours, checking every now and then. The tomatoes should be slightly shrunken but still brilliantly red after cooking (if they are too dark, they will taste bitter).

Serve topped with fresh basil leaves as an accompaniment to grills and fish, or use on top of bruschetta.

These bell peppers are a vegetable and pasta course in one. They should be luscious and soft, with a wrinkled browned exterior. The garlicky cherry tomatoes keep the pasta moist, and the pepper flakes and pecorino Romano give a hint of sharpness. A delicious antipasto and also a good accompaniment for fish.

roast bell peppers stuffed *with pasta and tomatoes*

4 medium yellow or red bell peppers

2 oz. *capelli d'angelo* or very fine spaghetti, about 1 cup

¹/₃ cup extra virgin olive oil

12 ripe cherry tomatoes, quartered

2 garlic cloves, finely chopped

¹/₄ cup chopped fresh basil leaves

¹/₂ cup pine nuts, coarsely chopped

¹/₂ teaspoon dried hot red pepper flakes (optional)

1 cup freshly grated pecorino Romano cheese

sea salt and freshly ground black pepper

a baking dish, lightly oiled

serves 4

Slice the tops off the bell peppers and reserve. Scrape out and discard all the seeds and white pith. Set the peppers upright in a lightly oiled dish small enough to fit them snugly. If they don't stand upright, shave a little piece off the bottom, but not right through.

Cook the pasta in plenty of boiling salted water until just *al dente*, about 8 minutes or according to the package instructions. Drain well and toss with 2 tablespoons of the olive oil.

Put the tomatoes in a bowl with another 2 tablespoons of oil, the garlic, basil, pine nuts, pepper flakes, if using, and pecorino and mix well. Season to taste with salt and pepper. Add the pasta to the peppers, filling them by two-thirds, then spoon in the tomato mixture. Put the pepper lids on top and brush liberally all over with the remaining olive oil.

Bake in a preheated oven at 425°F for 25–30 minutes or until the peppers start to wrinkle and blister. Serve hot or at room temperature.

My favorite recipe for sweet peppers is this one from Sicily. I never use green ones because I find them too bitter—they are just unripe red bell peppers and you need all that Mediterranean sunshine and sweetness trapped inside the red and yellow ones. When cooked, the peppers should be very soft and well caramelized for this recipe to be properly successful. Delicious on its own, this dish will also be great with a grilled steak.

sautéed bell peppers *with olives and capers*

⅓ cup extra virgin olive oil

2 medium red bell peppers, cut in half, seeded, and cut into thin strips

2 medium yellow bell peppers, cut in half, seeded, and cut into thin strips

4 garlic cloves, thinly sliced

6 anchovy fillets in oil, drained

3 tablespoons wine vinegar

2 tablespoons salted capers, rinsed and soaked in water for 10 minutes, then drained

½ cup mixed whole black and green olives

sea salt and freshly ground black pepper

serves 4

Heat the oil in a large skillet. Add the bell peppers and garlic cloves and cook over fairly high heat for 10 minutes, stirring often to prevent burning, until they start to caramelize. Alternatively, you can do this all in a roasting pan in a hot oven, roasting them at 425°F for about 20 minutes, turning once. However, I would keep the garlic cloves whole in this case to prevent them burning.

When well caramelized, stir in the anchovies and cook, stirring for about 2 minutes until they dissolve. Add the vinegar and stir-fry for a few minutes to let the flavors develop and the vinegar evaporate. Finally, stir in the capers and olives and continue to cook for a couple of minutes until heated through. Add salt and pepper to taste, then serve hot or at room temperature.

Funghetto (as this dish is known in Italian) has nothing to do with mushrooms, despite what its name might suggest. It refers to a method of cooking involving a lot of hot oil. Sautéing cubed eggplant concentrates the flavor and creates a lovely crust.

golden eggplant
with tomatoes and capers

2 medium eggplant

3 tablespoons salt

sunflower or olive oil, for cooking

2 tablespoons tomato puree or sun-dried tomato puree, or 1 tablespoon tomato paste

1 tablespoon small capers in vinegar, drained

3 tablespoons chopped fresh flat-leaf parsley

2 garlic cloves, very finely chopped

sea salt and freshly ground black pepper

serves 4

Trim the eggplant and cut into bite-size cubes, about ¾ inch square. Half fill a large bowl with cold water and stir in the salt until dissolved. Add the eggplant and put a plate on top to hold them under the water. Set aside for 30 minutes, then remove the plate and drain through a colander. Rinse under cold water, then dry very well on a clean, lintfree dishtowel or with paper towels.

Pour ½ inch depth of oil into a wok or large skillet. Heat until a piece of bread will sizzle instantly when it hits the oil. Cook the eggplant in batches until deep golden brown, about 5 minutes, then drain on paper towels.

Dilute the tomato puree with ¼ cup water and add the capers. Pour into a large skillet, bring to a boil, add the eggplant, and toss well to coat with the tomato. Add salt and pepper to taste. Mix the parsley and garlic together in a small bowl. Pile the eggplant into a warm dish, sprinkle with the parsley and garlic mixture, and serve hot or warm.

My friend Louise, who lives in Italy, goes completely crazy for this dish. She always persuades me to put it on the menu for my guests on our cooking course in Tuscany, but it's really for her. It is very rich and deserves to be eaten on its own. It is said to originate in Campania and is often confused with *melanzane alla Parmigiana*—another dish entirely.

baked eggplant, tomato, mozzarella, and parmesan

4 medium eggplant

2 tablespoons olive oil, plus extra for the eggplant

1 small onion, finely chopped

two 14½-oz. cans chopped tomatoes, drained

2 tablespoons chopped fresh basil leaves

½–¾ cup freshly grated Parmesan cheese

8 oz. fresh mozzarella cheese, thinly sliced, about 2 cups

sea salt and freshly ground black pepper

a shallow oven dish, 10 inches diameter, lightly oiled

serves 4

Cut the eggplant lengthwise into strips ½ inch wide. Soak them for 30 minutes in a bowl of heavily salted water.

Heat the oil in a skillet, add the onion, and cook for 5 minutes until softening, then add the tomatoes and basil and simmer gently for 30 minutes. Season with salt and pepper.

Drain the eggplant, then rinse and pat dry. Sauté them or brush with olive oil and roast in a preheated oven at 350°F for about 20 minutes until deep golden brown. Set aside.

Arrange the eggplant in a single layer in the oven dish, then add a layer of grated Parmesan, followed by a layer of sliced mozzarella and a layer of the tomato sauce. Continue layering in this order until all the ingredients have been used, ending with a sauce layer (this will keep the dish moist—if you want a crisp top, end with eggplant and Parmesan).

Bake in the oven at 350°F for 30–35 minutes until browned and bubbling. Remove and set aside for 10 minutes to settle before serving. Serve warm or at room temperature.

Zucchini are much more flavorful when cooked this way—bathed in garlic and olive oil, then stuffed with sweet, ripe cherry tomatoes and enveloped in melting fontina cheese. Delightfully fresh and summery.

baked zucchini and tomatoes *with fontina*

Cut the zucchini in half lengthwise and trim a little off the uncut sides so that they will sit still like boats. Using a teaspoon, scoop out the soft-seeded centers and discard, then arrange the zucchini boats in a row in the prepared dish.

Put the garlic, olive oil, salt, and pepper in a bowl, stir well, then brush over the cut surfaces of the zucchini. Arrange the halved tomatoes in the hollowed "boats," season well, then sprinkle with olive oil and bread crumbs. Bake in a preheated oven at 350°F for 30 minutes.

Remove from the oven and arrange the cheese over the zucchini and tomatoes. Return the dish to the oven for another 10–15 minutes to melt the cheese. Serve immediately while the cheese is still bubbling.

6 medium zucchini
(as straight as possible)

2 garlic cloves, chopped

2 tablespoons olive oil,
plus extra for sprinkling

about 30 cherry tomatoes,
cut in half

3–4 tablespoons dry
bread crumbs

8 oz. fontina cheese, sliced,
about 2 cups

sea salt and freshly ground
black pepper

*a shallow ovenproof dish,
greased*

serves 6

sautéed zucchini
with pancetta and thyme

The saltiness of pancetta or bacon is the perfect partner for zucchini, which are sweet, though they can be a little mild. The mixture of pancetta and thyme really brings out their flavor, as long as you cook it all over high heat to concentrate the juices and stop the zucchini becoming too wet.

Trim the zucchini and cut into cubes. Heat the oil in a skillet, add the pancetta, and sauté until golden. Add the zucchini and sauté over brisk heat for 3–4 minutes, tossing them around the pan from time to time until the cut sides start to turn golden.

When golden, add the thyme and plenty of black pepper (you probably won't need any salt). Season with a squeeze of lemon juice and serve immediately.

1 lb. zucchini

3 tablespoons olive oil

½ cup pancetta cubes (cubed Italian bacon or prosciutto) or lardons

1 tablespoon chopped fresh thyme

sea salt (optional) and freshly ground black pepper

freshly squeezed juice of ½ lemon

serves 4

fennel and leeks braised in cream and lemon

Fennel bulbs take on a completely different character when cooked slowly. They are soft and creamy with a very mild anise flavor more akin to celery. Sweet leeks balance it nicely, and the cream and lemon transform this into a very soothing dish. I like to serve this recipe with summery white fish dishes or chicken with a few extra fennel seeds and lemon zest toasted in olive oil sprinkled on top.

Trim the stalks, fronds, and root ends from the fennel bulbs. Reserve any tender stalks and fronds and chop them to use for serving. Cut the bulbs into 4–6 wedges. Cook in boiling salted water for 10 minutes, then drain.

Trim the leeks, cut into thick rings, and rinse in cold water to remove any grit. Melt the butter in a shallow braising pan or deep skillet with a lid. When foaming, add the leeks and sauté over brisk heat for 1 minute. Add the fennel seeds, if using, then the lemon juice, lemon zest, and wine, bring to a boil, and boil hard until reduced by half. Tuck in the fennel so it nestles into the leeks.

Put the cream, milk, and grated nutmeg in a bowl, add salt and pepper to taste, stir well, then pour it over the fennel and leeks. Slowly bring to a boil, then turn down the heat, cover, and simmer very gently for about 35 minutes or until the fennel is tender at the thickest part. Serve immediately, sprinkled with any reserved chopped fennel fronds.

Note To cook in the oven, cover the dish with foil and bake for 35–40 minutes at 375°F.

2 medium fennel bulbs

2 large or 4 medium leeks (about 1½ cups after trimming)

4 tablespoons unsalted butter

1 teaspoon fennel seeds (optional)

finely grated zest and juice of 1 unwaxed lemon

2 tablespoons white wine or dry vermouth

1 cup heavy cream

1 cup milk

freshly grated nutmeg

sea salt and freshly ground black pepper

serves 4

Carrots are electric orange in Sicily and taste fantastic. Sicily is also the home of Marsala, which comes in all varieties from bone dry to rich and sweet, and I wish this selection were more widely available outside the home country. The nuttiness of the dry Marsala cooks into the sweet carrots, transforming them into something very special indeed. This old recipe is almost a version of French Vichy Carrots, with olive oil taking the place of the usual butter.

carrots *with olive oil and marsala*

1¼ lb. carrots, peeled, or scraped if young

3 large garlic cloves, unpeeled

6 tablespoons extra virgin olive oil

1¼ cups dry Marsala wine (or ½ cup dry sherry mixed with ¾ cup sweet Marsala wine)

sea salt and freshly ground black pepper

2 tablespoons chopped fresh flat-leaf parsley, to serve

serves 6

Slice the carrots into thin discs or into sticks. Rinse well and pat dry. Crush the garlic cloves to open them up, but don't crush to a pulp. Heat the oil in a heavy skillet until just warm, add the garlic, and sauté gently for 5 minutes until lightly golden. This will flavor the oil without too much harsh garlic taste. Remove and discard the garlic.

Add the carrots and cook over medium heat for 2–3 minutes, tossing them around occasionally. Pour in the Marsala, bring to a boil, then turn down to a simmer, cover, and cook until the carrots are tender (about 10 minutes, depending on thickness). By this time, the Marsala will have emulsified with the olive oil to make a thin sauce—if there seems to be too much, lift out the carrots and boil the sauce hard to reduce. Taste and season with salt and pepper. Transfer to a serving dish, top with the parsley, and serve.

Someone once said that life is too short to stuff a mushroom: wrong! The light stuffing in this recipe complements the mushroom's rich meaty flavor. If using a cultivated type, add a shake of wild mushroom powder to the caps before you add the stuffing.

ricotta-stuffed mushrooms

6 large mushroom caps, such as portobello, flat open mushrooms, or porcini, approximately 1 lb.

2 tablespoons olive oil, plus extra for brushing

2 garlic cloves, finely chopped

3 tablespoons chopped fresh flat-leaf parsley

½ cup black olives, pitted and chopped

3 sun-dried tomatoes, sliced

a pinch of ground hot red pepper

8 oz. fresh ricotta cheese, about 1 cup

sea salt and freshly ground black pepper

3 tablespoons freshly grated Parmesan or pecorino Romano cheese, to serve

a baking tray, oiled

serves 6

Pull the stalks off the mushrooms and chop the stalks finely. Heat the oil in a skillet and add the chopped stalks, garlic, parsley, and olives, and sauté for a couple of minutes to soften the garlic. Remove from the heat and transfer to a bowl. Stir in the tomatoes, hot red pepper, salt, and pepper, then stir in the ricotta very briefly—it must not be smooth.

Brush the mushroom caps all over with olive oil and arrange open-side up on the baking tray. Spoon the filling into the mushrooms in loose mounds. Sprinkle with the grated cheese and bake in a preheated oven at 375°F for 15–20 minutes or until the tops are pale golden. Serve immediately.

potato and mushroom gratin

2 lb. medium potatoes, about 6–8

1½ lb. flavorsome mushrooms such as portobello (or use fresh wild mushrooms)

extra virgin olive oil, for sprinkling

3½ cups stale (not dry) white bread crumbs

¼ cup freshly grated Parmesan cheese

¼ cup chopped fresh flat-leaf parsley

sea salt and freshly ground black pepper

a deep gratin or other ovenproof dish, well buttered

serves 4

Baking sliced potatoes and mushrooms in layers lets the potatoes absorb the juices and earthy flavor of the mushrooms. Try to use the darkest mushrooms you can find—they will have the best taste. You can always mix fresh ones with reconstituted dried mushrooms for a more intense flavor.

Peel the potatoes and slice thickly, putting them in a bowl of cold water as you go. Trim the mushrooms and slice thickly. Put half the potatoes in a layer in the bottom of the dish, sprinkle with olive oil, and cover with half the mushrooms.

Put the bread crumbs, Parmesan, parsley, salt, and pepper in a bowl and mix well. Spread half this mixture over the mushrooms, then sprinkle with more olive oil. Cover with a layer of potatoes, sprinkle with olive oil, then add a layer of the remaining mushrooms. Finally, sprinkle with the remaining bread crumb mixture and more oil.

Cover with foil and bake in a preheated oven at 350°F for 30 minutes. Uncover and cook for another 30 minutes until the potatoes are tender and the top is golden brown.

Note If you blanch the potato slices first for 5 minutes in boiling salted water, they will take only 30 minutes to cook.

A treat for potato and chile lovers, this dish is simplicity itself. It is important to use a good olive oil because it is very much a part of the dish. I use large new potatoes, which have an almost creamy texture and absorb the olive oil well. However, you can use any potatoes—it will work with almost anything.

the devil's potatoes

1 lb. large new potatoes, unpeeled, about 3–4

2 fresh red chiles

1 cup fruity olive oil

sea salt and freshly ground black pepper

serves 4

Boil the potatoes whole in a large saucepan of salted water.

While they are boiling, cut the chiles in half lengthwise, remove the seeds, and chop the flesh finely (wear rubber gloves to protect your fingers if you like). Heat the olive oil very gently in a small skillet and add the chiles—they should delicately fizzle when added. Stir briefly, then remove from the heat. Add salt and pepper to taste.

When the potatoes are cooked, drain, then when cool enough to handle, slice thickly and arrange half the slices in a single layer on a serving dish. Pour half the chile oil over the potatoes, then top with the remaining potatoes and pour the remaining oil over them. Cover with aluminum foil and let stand for 10 minutes before serving with a little extra salt and pepper. They should be served warm.

Any type of dried bean will work here—only the cooking times will differ. To make sure that the onion isn't too strong, soak the slices in cold water for 10 minutes. Alternatively, you could blanch them for 1 minute in boiling water, to which a squeeze of lemon juice has been added.

cannellini beans *with olive oil and mint*

Soak the beans overnight in about 8 cups cold water. The next day, drain and put them in a large saucepan. Add the garlic cloves, the whole mint leaves, and pepper. Cover with cold water, slowly bring to a boil, then turn down the heat and simmer for 25–30 minutes until tender. Times will vary according to the freshness of the beans. Drain well and remove the garlic and mint.

Put the olive oil, chopped mint, and onion in a bowl and mix with a fork. Add the drained beans and toss them carefully with the dressing. Taste and check the seasoning—you may have to add salt—and serve warm or at room temperature.

2 1/2 cups dried white beans, such as cannellini or navy beans

2 garlic cloves, unpeeled but smashed open

6–8 whole mint leaves, plus 3 tablespoons chopped or torn mint leaves

1/3 cup extra virgin olive oil

1 small red onion, thinly sliced into rings or half moons

sea salt and freshly ground black pepper

serves 4

A rich, wintry stew of lentils, onions, and herbs—perfect to serve with game dishes, duck, and of course, meaty Italian sausages. Sometimes, it is even better served on its own with a stack of grilled bread, rubbed with garlic and sprinkled with olive oil, as a filling supper dish in front of a crackling log fire. Red wine is the only accompaniment you'll need.

12 small pearl onions

2 tablespoons olive oil

2 oz. pancetta cubes or lardons, about ½ cup

2 carrots, finely chopped

2 celery stalks, finely chopped

3 garlic cloves, finely chopped

3 bay leaves

2–3 sprigs of thyme

a sprig of rosemary

2 cups brown lentils

½ cup light dry red wine

1 tablespoon balsamic vinegar

3 tablespoons chopped fresh flat-leaf parsley

2 tablespoons unsalted butter

sea salt and freshly ground black pepper

serves 6

lentils braised
with little onions and herbs

To peel the onions, put them in a bowl and cover with boiling water. Leave for 2–3 minutes, then drain. Peel off the loosened skins while they are still warm, leaving the onions whole. Trim the root end, but not completely, because this will hold them together.

Heat the oil in a saucepan or casserole dish and add the pancetta. Let cook slowly for 5 minutes to release the fat, then add the carrots, celery, and garlic. Stir well and cook over medium heat for about 5 minutes until beginning to soften. Add the bay leaves, thyme, rosemary, onions, lentils, wine, and vinegar. Cook over high heat for 1 minute, then add enough water to cover everything completely. Season to taste with salt and pepper. Bring to a boil, turn down the heat, cover, and simmer gently for about 40 minutes until the lentils are completely soft and they have absorbed most of the liquid.

Remove the pan from the heat and remove and discard the herbs. Stir in the chopped fresh parsley and the butter. Serve immediately.

fish

1 lb. small squid, cleaned

8 raw shrimp (optional)

2 lb. fresh mussels and clams*

3½ lb. mixed whole but cleaned fish (see note on fish choice)

flavored broth

⅔ cup extra virgin olive oil

4 medium leeks, sliced and well washed

4 garlic cloves, finely chopped

1¼ cups dry white wine

a large pinch of saffron threads

½ lb. ripe red plum tomatoes, coarsely chopped

2 tablespoons sun-dried tomato paste or 6 sun-dried tomatoes in oil, drained and coarsely chopped

1 teaspoon fennel seeds

1 tablespoon dried oregano

sea salt and freshly ground black pepper

to serve

lemon wedges

handfuls of chopped fresh flat-leaf parsley

crusty bread

serves 6–8

Scrub and debeard the mussels. Tap any open mussels and clams against the counter. Discard any that don't close—they are dead— and also any with damaged shells. Keep in a bowl of cold water until ready to cook.

This stew is the perfect family feast. A well-flavored base broth is essential, including saffron and fennel seeds, and the fish is then poached in this stock. The fish is served separately and the broth is ladled on top.

a big fish stew

To make the broth, heat the olive oil in a large, heavy pot and add the leeks and garlic. Cook gently for about 5 minutes until softened. Pour in the white wine and boil rapidly until reduced by half. Add the saffron, tomatoes, tomato paste, fennel seeds, and oregano. Pour in 2¾ cups water and bring to a boil. Turn down the heat, cover, and simmer for 20 minutes until the tomatoes and oil separate.

Start cooking the fish. Add the squid to the pot and poach for 3–4 minutes. Remove with a slotted spoon, put on a plate, cover, and keep them warm. Add the shrimp, if using, and simmer just until opaque. Remove with a slotted spoon and keep warm with the squid. Add the mussels and clams to the broth, cover, and boil for a few minutes until they open. Remove with a slotted spoon and keep them warm. Discard any that haven't opened.

Poach all the remaining fish until just cooked, remove from the broth, arrange on a serving dish, and set the mussels, squid, and shrimp on top. Taste the broth, which will have all the flavors of the cooked fish in it, and add salt and pepper if necessary. Moisten the fish with some broth and serve the rest separately with the lemon wedges, parsley, and lots of crusty bread.

Fish choice Choose at least 4 varieties—the greater the variety, the more intense the flavor. Do not choose oily fish like salmon or bluefish. Choose from: cod, grouper, halibut, monkfish, sea bass, shark, swordfish, tilefish, whiting, or lobster.

fish baked in a salt crust

This excellent method of cooking fish conserves
the juices without in any way oversalting the flesh.
The salt bakes hard to form a protective crust so
that the fish cooks in its own juices—the skin
protects it from the salt. It's a nice idea to stuff
the cavity with fresh herbs and sliced lemon before
burying the fish in salt.

at least 2 lb. sea salt

1 egg white

2-4 lb. whole large
firm-fleshed fish, cleaned
but not scaled

a tomato salad, to serve

*a long ovenproof dish
(choose one that will
comfortably hold the
whole fish)*

serves 4–6

Pour enough salt into the dish to make a layer 1 inch thick. Mix the egg white with 3 tablespoons water and sprinkle half the liquid over the salt. Set the fish on the salt bed and pour enough salt around and over it to cover it completely. Sprinkle with the remaining egg white and water.

Bake the fish in a preheated oven at 375°F for 45 minutes to 1 hour.

Remove from the oven and put the dish, with the fish still encased in its snowy armor, in the middle of the table.

Crack open the salt crust with a rolling pin. Remove the shards of salt crust and peel back the skin to reveal perfectly cooked, succulent flesh without a trace of saltiness. Serve with a simple tomato salad.

When opened up and boned, sardines cook in minutes in a hot oven. Marinating them in oil and lemon juice lends piquancy to the delicate flesh. This is a good dish to prepare a day ahead, then serve for lunch with salad.

sardines baked *with garlic, lemon, olive oil, and bread crumbs*

Scale the sardines with the blunt edge of a knife. Cut off the heads and slit open the bellies. Remove the guts under running water. Slide your thumb along the backbone to release the flesh along its length. Take hold of the backbone at the head end and lift it out. The fish should now be open flat like a book.

Put the oil, lemon zest, and juice in a large bowl, beat well, then stir in the garlic, parsley, capers, salt, and pepper. Holding each sardine by the tail, dip in the lemony olive oil, then put skin side up in the ovenproof dish. Pour in any remaining liquid, sprinkle with the bread crumbs, and bake in a preheated oven at 400°F for 15 minutes.

Serve warm immediately, or let cool, then store overnight in the refrigerator. Serve the next day at room temperature, when the sardines will have marinated in the oil, lemon, and herbs. Add the parsley and lemon wedges, then serve.

8 fresh whole sardines

1/3 cup good olive oil

finely grated zest and juice of 1 unwaxed lemon

2 garlic cloves, thinly sliced

3 tablespoons chopped fresh flat-leaf parsley, plus extra to serve

1 tablespoon salted capers, rinsed, drained, and chopped

3 tablespoons dried bread crumbs

sea salt and freshly ground black pepper

lemon wedges, to serve

a shallow ovenproof dish

serves 4

Sea bass has a wonderful, clean, fresh taste and baking in parchment is the best way to cook whole fish (with the possible exception of grilling over embers). The parchment lets the fish steam in its own juices, absorbing the aroma of the fresh herbs and lemon. This cooking time should be perfect—the fish is better slightly underdone at the bone than overdone. The wrapped fish should be opened at the table to appreciate the full aroma.

sea bass baked in parchment

Cut 2 large rectangles of parchment paper big enough to wrap each fish generously. Brush the rectangles with a little oil.

Season the cavities of the fish with salt and pepper. Put 2 bay leaves in each one and tuck in the thyme and lemon slices.

Put one fish on one half of the paper, sprinkle with white wine or lemon juice, fold the other half over loosely, and twist or fold the edges tightly together to seal. Repeat with the other fish, then put both wrapped fish on the baking tray.

Bake in a preheated oven at 375°F for 20 minutes. Serve immediately, opening the wrapped fish at the table.

2 sea bass, about 12 oz. each, cleaned and scaled

about 1 tablespoon olive oil

4 fresh bay leaves

2 sprigs of thyme

6 thin slices of lemon

about 2 tablespoons dry white wine or freshly squeezed lemon juice

sea salt and freshly ground black pepper

a baking tray

serves 2

This dish originated in Venice during the Renaissance and has been cooked and served on gondolas on the eve of the Feast of the Redeemer in July ever since. As well as adding flavor to the delicate fish, the marinade slightly preserves it too. This dish can also be made with sardines, but sole is popular in Venice.

fillets of sole *in sweet and sour onion marinade*

8 sole fillets, skinned

all-purpose flour, for dusting

½ cup olive oil

sea salt and freshly ground black pepper

sweet and sour marinade

¼ cup olive oil

2 mild onions, thinly sliced

3 bay leaves or a sprig

¼ cup white wine vinegar

to serve

salad

crusty bread

serves 4

To make the marinade, heat the olive oil in a skillet over medium heat. Add the onions and bay leaves. Cook, stirring, for 15–20 minutes. The onions should be softened and translucent and not browned at all. Add the vinegar and boil rapidly for a few minutes until amalgamated with the onion juices. Remove from the heat, pour into a bowl, and set aside.

Season the sole fillets with salt, and dip them in flour to coat both sides, shaking to remove the excess. Heat the olive oil in a skillet and cook the sole fillets for about 1 minute on each side. Remove and drain on paper towels.

Spoon half of the cooked and cooled marinade into a shallow dish, season with pepper, and arrange the sole fillets on top. Pour in the remaining marinade, cover with plastic wrap, and let marinate for several hours or overnight in the refrigerator. Serve at room temperature with a salad and some crusty bread.

Fresh tuna bakes very well in the oven, especially
if marinated first to keep it moist. I have taken the
liberty of adding capers and mint to the traditional
salmoriglio sauce adored by Sicilians. The capers add
a sharp edge to the sauce, and cut through the
richness of the fish.

oven-baked tuna *with salsa*

3 tablespoons good olive oil

4 garlic cloves, crushed

1 teaspoon dried oregano

¼ cup dry white wine

1 lemon, thinly sliced

4 thick tuna steaks, 6–8 oz. each

sea salt and freshly ground
black pepper

caper and mint salsa

1 tablespoon salted capers,
drained

2 tablespoons red wine vinegar

1–2 teaspoons sugar

finely grated zest and juice of
½ unwaxed lemon

¼ cup good olive oil

1 garlic clove, finely chopped

2 tablespoons finely chopped
fresh mint leaves

a non-aluminum ovenproof dish

serves 4

Put the olive oil, garlic, oregano, wine, salt, and pepper in a bowl
and stir well. Spread half the lemon slices in the ovenproof dish
and put the tuna steaks on top. Pour the olive oil mixture over
them and put the remaining lemon slices on top. Set aside for
30 minutes.

Meanwhile, to make the salsa, soak the capers in water for
10 minutes, drain, pat dry, and chop if large. Put the vinegar and
sugar in a bowl and stir until the sugar has dissolved. Add the
lemon zest and juice. Beat in the olive oil, then add the garlic,
chopped mint, and capers. Set aside to infuse.

Bake the tuna in a preheated oven at 350°F for about 12 minutes.
The fish should be just cooked in the center—it can be served
slightly pink. Lift onto warm plates, leaving the juices behind.
Serve with the salsa spooned on top.

Tuna is a very rich meat and is always cut thinly in Italy—never as the thick seared steaks we are used to. Marinating the slices in mustard and grappa gives them a piquant crust—so good with the sweet bell peppers.

grilled tuna steaks *with peperonata*

To make the marinade, crush the garlic, put in a bowl, and beat in the mustard and grappa. Season with salt and pepper and use to spread over the cut sides of the tuna. Arrange in a non-metal dish, cover, and let marinate in a cool place for about 1 hour.

To make the peperonata, heat 3 tablespoons of the oil in a saucepan, then add the tomatoes and pepper flakes. Cook over medium heat for 10 minutes, or until the tomatoes disintegrate.

Heat the remaining oil in a skillet, add the onions, garlic, and peppers, and sauté for about 10 minutes until softening. Add the pepper mixture to the tomatoes and simmer, covered, for 45 minutes until very soft. Taste and season with salt and pepper.

Preheat the broiler or a grill. Sprinkle the steaks with olive oil and arrange on a rack over a foil-lined broiler pan. Broil for about 2 minutes on each side until crusty on the outside and still pink in the middle. Alternatively, grill over hot embers for slightly less time. Serve with the peperonata, which can be served hot or cold.

4 tuna loin steaks cut $\frac{1}{2}$ inch thick

olive oil, for cooking

sea salt and freshly ground black pepper

marinade

4 garlic cloves

3 tablespoons Dijon mustard

2 tablespoons grappa or brandy

peperonata

$\frac{1}{3}$ cup olive oil

2 lb. fresh ripe tomatoes, peeled, cut in half, seeded, and chopped, or two 14$\frac{1}{2}$-oz. cans chopped tomatoes

$\frac{1}{2}$ teaspoon hot red pepper flakes

2 medium onions, thinly sliced

3 garlic cloves, chopped

3 large red bell peppers, cut in half, seeded, and cut into thin strips

serves 4

meat and poultry

chicken roasted *with bay leaves, lemon, and garlic*

A memorable way of roasting a chicken—all the flavors permeate the flesh during its time in the oven, and the smell in the kitchen is wonderful. This dish is particularly good eaten cold, at a picnic.

Starting at the vent end of the chicken, slide your hand carefully underneath the skin of each breast to loosen it. Push 3 or 4 slices of lemon under the skin of each breast, slide the garlic slices on top of the lemon, then finish with 3 bay leaves on each side. Smooth down the skin. Rub with olive oil, then salt and pepper.

Arrange a bed of bay leaves in the roasting pan and put the remaining lemon slices over them. Put the chicken on top and roast in a preheated oven at 375°F for 20 minutes per pound, plus 20 minutes extra, basting every now and then, until golden brown, crisp, and cooked through. To check, push a skewer into the thickest part of the thigh—the juices should run clear and golden. If there is any trace of pink, cook for 5–10 minutes longer and check again.

Serve hot, or cool, chill, and serve cold.

1 free-range chicken, about 3 lb.

1 lemon, very thinly sliced

3 garlic cloves, thinly sliced

6 small fresh bay leaves (or use sage or even basil), plus extra bay leaves to make a bed

a little olive oil

sea salt and freshly ground black pepper

a roasting pan

serves 6

A magnificent way to cook lamb long and slowly, especially if it is not as young as it might be. Liver is often served with onions cooked to melting sweetness, and this is a similar technique. The black olives enrich the dish and give it a smoky taste. The chops can be finished off in a medium hot oven instead of cooking on top. They are good reheated.

braised lamb chops
with onions, herbs, and olives

Season the meat on both sides with salt and pepper.

Heat half the oil in a large sauté pan or heavy skillet until very hot, then add the chops and quickly brown on both sides. Remove to a plate and let cool.

Heat the remaining oil in the same pan and add the onions. Cook gently for 15 minutes, stirring occasionally, until the onions begin to soften—do not let them brown. Stir in the herbs, anchovies, olives, salt, and pepper.

Arrange the chops on top of the bed of onions and cover with a lid. Cook over very low heat for 20 minutes, watching that the onions don't catch and burn. Serve topped with rosemary sprigs.

8–12 lamb chops, depending on size

½ cup olive oil

2 lb. onions, thinly sliced

2 tablespoons chopped fresh oregano and rosemary, mixed

4 anchovies in oil, drained, rinsed, and chopped

15 black olives, pitted

sea salt and freshly ground black pepper

rosemary sprigs, to serve

serves 4

leg of lamb

This leg of lamb is braised until cooked and tender, then roasted to color it. The powerful flavorings melt into the meat, with the anchovies disappearing to leave a salty note. This way of cooking lamb stems from the Roman Empire, when the most popular condiment was a sauce made from fermented fish.

3 lb. leg of lamb

2 tablespoons olive oil

10 juniper berries

3 garlic cloves, crushed

2 oz. canned anchovies

1 tablespoon chopped fresh rosemary

2 tablespoons balsamic vinegar

2 sprigs of rosemary

2 fresh bay leaves

1¼ cups dry white wine

sprigs of fresh thyme

sea salt and freshly ground black pepper

a flameproof casserole dish (into which the lamb should fit snugly)

serves 6

Trim the lamb of any excess fat. Heat the oil in the casserole dish, add the lamb, and brown it all over. Remove and cool quickly.

Crush 6 of the juniper berries, the garlic, anchovies, and chopped rosemary with a mortar and pestle. Stir in the vinegar and mix to a paste. Using a small, sharp knife, make many small incisions into the lamb. Spread the paste all over the meat, working it into the incisions, then season with salt and pepper.

Put the rosemary sprigs and bay leaves in the casserole dish and set the lamb on top. Pour in the wine. Crush the remaining juniper berries and add to the lamb, then add the thyme. Cover, bring to a boil on top of the stove, then place in a preheated oven at 325°F and braise for 1 hour, turning the lamb every 20 minutes.

Raise the oven temperature to 400°F. Roast uncovered for another 45 minutes or until browned—the lamb should be very tender and cooked through.

Transfer the lamb to a serving dish and keep it warm. Skim off the fat from the pan, then boil the sauce, adding a little water if necessary and scraping up the sediment. Season with salt and pepper if necessary and serve with the lamb.

pork loin roasted
with rosemary and garlic

This is a classic oven-baked Tuscan dish. Redolent of the early morning markets where *porchetta* is sold crammed into huge buns, this dish recreates all those tastes and smells in your oven at home. Use plenty of rosemary in this dish.

Turn the pork loin fat-side down. Make deep slits all over, especially in the thick part. Put the garlic, rosemary, and at least a teaspoon of salt and pepper (more will give a truly authentic Tuscan flavor) into a food processor and blend to a paste. Push this paste into all the slits in the meat and spread the remainder over the surface of the meat. Roll up and tie with fine twine.

Weigh the meat and calculate the cooking time, allowing 25 minutes for every pound. At this stage you can cover it with plastic wrap and chill for several hours to deepen the flavor. When ready to cook, preheat the oven to 450°F, or as high as your oven will go. Uncover the pork and brown all over in a hot skillet. Transfer the pork to a roasting pan, then pour the wine over it and tuck in the rosemary sprigs.

Roast for 20 minutes. Turn down the heat to 400°F, and roast for the remaining calculated time, basting the pork loin every 20 minutes.

Remove the pork from the oven and let rest in a warm place for 15 minutes before carving into thick slices. Serve with the pan juices.

1 boneless center-cut pork loin roast (about 3 lb.)

6 large garlic cloves

¼ cup chopped fresh rosemary

1¼ cups dry white wine

sprigs of fresh rosemary

olive oil, for brushing

sea salt and freshly ground black pepper

2 roasting pans

serves 6

beefsteak *with arugula*

Italians love meat cooked very rare: you will often see a slip of a girl tucking into a steak that would comfortably feed two—and she will eat it all. The steaks are produced from the huge, handsome, white Chianina cattle, native to Tuscany.

Brush the steaks with olive oil and season very well with salt and pepper. Heat a stovetop grill pan or light an outdoor grill. When the pan is smoking hot, add the steaks and cook for 2 minutes on each side to seal, then lower the heat and continue to cook for about 4 minutes per side for medium-rare steaks, less for rare.

Transfer the steaks to a cutting board and slice them thickly. Put a pile of arugula on 4 warm plates and arrange the sliced meat on top. Pour any juices from the steaks onto the meat and serve immediately, topped with chopped parsley.

4 sirloin steaks, about 8 oz. each

2 tablespoons olive oil

8 oz. arugula, about 4 large handfuls

sea salt and freshly ground black pepper

chopped fresh flat-leaf parsley, to serve

serves 4

2 bottles Barolo or other good-quality red wine, 750 ml each

3 lb. boneless stewing beef, such as chuck, or bottom round, well trimmed

2 onions, coarsely chopped

2 carrots, chopped

1 celery stalk, chopped

2 bay leaves

2 large sprigs of thyme

6 peppercorns

2 allspice berries, crushed

3 tablespoons olive oil

2 tablespoons tomato paste

about 6 cups beef broth, to cover

sea salt and freshly ground black pepper

chopped fresh flat-leaf parsley, to serve

a large flameproof casserole dish

serves 6–8

Cut the meat into very large chunks—long, slow cooking tenderizes it perfectly. Served with boiled potatoes and green vegetables, this is a good dish for a crowd.

beef braised in red wine

Pour the wine into a large saucepan and bring to a boil. Boil hard until reduced by half (leaving 3 cups). Let cool completely.

Cut the meat into 2-inch pieces. Put in a large plastic bag with the onions, carrots, celery, bay leaves, thyme, peppercorns, and allspice. Pour in the cooled wine. Shake the bag to mix, then seal the bag and put it in a large bowl to marinate in the refrigerator overnight.

Open the bag and pour the contents into a colander set over a bowl. Separate the meat from the vegetable mixture and pat the meat pieces dry with paper towels. Reserve the wine.

Heat the oil in the casserole dish on top of the stove and brown the meat well in batches. Return all the meat to the dish, then stir in the vegetable mixture. Add the reserved wine and stir in the tomato paste. Add enough broth to cover the meat and vegetables. Bring to a boil, reduce the heat, cover, and either simmer gently on the stove for 2–3 hours, or cook in a preheated oven at 325°F for 2–3 hours until very tender. Top up the liquid with extra broth if it evaporates too quickly.

Using a slotted spoon, transfer the meat to a bowl. Discard the bay leaves. Pour the sauce into a blender or food processor and blend until smooth (the sauce will look pale, but will darken when reheated). Add salt and pepper to taste. The sauce should be quite thick—if not, boil to reduce it. Stir the meat back into the sauce, reheat, sprinkle with parsley, and serve.

The Tuscans have a reputation for being great game hunters. In the past, when they used to cook little gamebirds, or *uccelletti*, they would generally season them with sage. This dish contains no *uccelletti*, but it is cooked in the same way—and uses sausages in place of the birds. The beans are also delicious served with roast pork—or even a homemade hamburger.

grilled sausages
with tomato and sage bean stew

2 ¼ cups dried cannellini or navy beans or other white beans, or, if lucky, 2 lb. fresh cannellini or borlotti beans in their pods

a pinch of baking soda

8 fat fresh Italian-style pork sausages

⅓ cup olive oil

3 garlic cloves, crushed

about 10 fresh sage leaves

12 oz. fresh ripe tomatoes, peeled, seeded, and pureed, about 1 ¼ cups

sea salt and freshly ground black pepper

serves 4

If using dried beans, cover with plenty of cold water and soak overnight. The next day, drain and rinse them, then cook in plenty of boiling water without any salt, but with a pinch of baking soda (to keep the skins soft) for about 1–1 ½ hours, or until tender. Drain. If using fresh beans, shell and boil them in slightly salted water until ready, 25–30 minutes, then drain.

Brush the sausages with oil and grill or broil for 15 minutes until tender and crisp on the outside.

Meanwhile, heat the oil in a saucepan and add the garlic, sage, and black pepper. Fry until the garlic is golden and the sage beginning to become transparent and crisp. Remove and reserve a few crisp leaves for serving.

Add the pureed tomatoes, heat to simmering, then add the cooked beans. Cook for 10 minutes, then taste and adjust the seasoning with salt and pepper. Serve the sausages with the beans and top with the reserved crisp sage leaves.

sweet things

It's worth making a journey to Italy just to taste lemons that have been properly ripened in the sun. Walk through a lemon grove when the glossy green trees are in blossom and the scent is intoxicating. The beautiful leaves can be used like bay leaves or the more exotic Thai lime leaves to impart a lemony flavor to sweet and savory dishes alike. I mix the orange with the lemon juice because it softens the acidity of some un-sunkissed lemons.

sorbetto al limone

1½ cups sugar

finely grated zest and juice of
6 unwaxed lemons, plus
6 medium, even-size lemons

finely grated zest and juice of
1 unwaxed orange

an ice cream maker

serves 6

Put the sugar and 2¾ cups water in a saucepan with the lemon and orange zest. Bring slowly to a boil and boil rapidly for 3–4 minutes. Remove from the heat and let cool. Meanwhile, strain the fruit juices into a bowl. When the syrup is cold, strain into the bowl of juice. Chill. When cold, churn it in an ice cream maker according to the manufacturer's instructions.

Meanwhile, cut the tops off the remaining 6 lemons and shave a little off each base so that it will stand up. Scoop out the insides (squeeze and keep the juice for another recipe). Put the hollowed lemons in the freezer. When the sorbet is frozen, fill the lemon shells with it and set the tops back on. Replace in the freezer until needed. Soften in the refrigerator for 10–15 minutes before serving.

mint sorbet

Italians are very fond of sweet and sticky liqueurs, so I have laced this *sorbetto* with crème de menthe—bliss.

1 1/2 cups sugar

2 cups dry white wine, such as sauvignon blanc, chilled

1 1/2 cups fresh mint leaves

2 tablespoons freshly squeezed lime juice

2–3 tablespoons crème de menthe liqueur

an ice cream maker

makes about 1 quart

Put the sugar and 2 cups water in a saucepan and bring slowly to a boil, stirring until the sugar dissolves. Remove from the heat, then stir in the wine and 1 cup of the mint leaves. Let cool, then chill for several hours. Strain the syrup into a blender. Add the remaining mint leaves, lime juice, and liqueur. Blend until the leaves disappear and the syrup is speckled green.

Pour into an ice cream maker and freeze according to the manufacturer's instructions. Transfer to a chilled freezer container, cover, and freeze until firm. Let soften in the refrigerator for 20 minutes before serving.

---

1 small, very ripe, orange-fleshed cantaloupe or charentais melon, about 2 1/2 lb., cut in half and seeded

2/3 cup sugar

3 tablespoons light corn syrup

1 tablespoon freshly squeezed lemon juice

3 cups whole milk

2/3 cup skimmed milk powder

1 teaspoon powdered gelatin

an ice cream maker

serves 8

cantaloupe melon ice cream

Use the ripest, most fragrant, orange-fleshed melon for this. Add a dash of melon liqueur if lacking in flavor.

Scoop out the melon flesh into a food processor or blender. Add the sugar, syrup, and lemon juice, and puree until smooth.

Pour the milk into a saucepan and beat in the dried milk powder and gelatin. Bring slowly to just below the boil. Stir in the melon puree and transfer to a bowl to cool. When cold, chill in the refrigerator for at least 1 hour or overnight.

When thoroughly chilled, transfer to an ice cream maker and freeze according to the manufacturer's instructions. Transfer to a chilled freezer container, cover, and freeze until firm. Let soften in the refrigerator for 20 minutes before serving.

watermelon sorbetto
with chocolate chip seeds

A beautiful pink, exotic *sorbetto* from Sicily, delicately perfumed with a hint of cinnamon. Just for fun, the chocolate chips are added to represent the black watermelon seeds, but they do give a nice crunchy texture.

1½ lb. red watermelon flesh, cut into cubes, about 4 cups

¾ cup sugar (or a bit less if the melon is very sweet)

1 small cinnamon stick

freshly squeezed juice of 2 ripe lemons

a little pink food coloring, if necessary

⅓ cup chocolate chips

an ice cream maker (optional)*

serves 4–6

*Freeze in an ice cream maker for the best results

Remove the seeds from the melon with the tip of a small knife. Put the flesh in a food processor and puree until smooth. With the machine running, pour in the sugar and blend for 30 seconds.

Pour the melon mixture into a saucepan and add the cinnamon stick. Slowly bring to a boil, stirring all the time to dissolve the sugar completely, then turn down the heat to a bare simmer for 1 minute. Remove from the heat, then add the lemon juice, and a few drops of pink food coloring if necessary.

Let cool. When cold, remove the cinnamon stick and chill the mixture in the refrigerator for at least 1 hour (or overnight—this makes freezing quicker).

Transfer to an ice cream maker and freeze according to the manufacturer's instructions. Stir in the chocolate chips when the sorbetto is still soft. Transfer to a chilled freezer container, cover, and freeze until firm. Let soften in the refrigerator for 20 minutes before serving.

Alternatively, pour into a shallow freezer tray and freeze until the sorbetto is frozen around the edges. Mash well with a fork. When it is half frozen again, blend in a food processor until creamy, stir in the chocolate chips, then cover and freeze until firm. Let soften in the refrigerator for 20 minutes before serving.

There is nothing quite as sensual as warm zabaglione served straight from the pan. Many like to beat it in a copper bowl so that it cooks quickly. The secret is not to let the mixture get too hot, but still hot enough to cook and thicken the egg yolks. It must be made at the last moment, but it doesn't take long and is well worth the effort.

zabaglione

2 large egg yolks

2 tablespoons sweet
Marsala wine

2 tablespoons sugar

savoiardi or ladyfingers,
for dipping

serves 2

Put the egg yolks, Marsala, and sugar in a medium heatproof bowl (preferably copper or stainless steel) and beat with an electric beater or a whisk until well blended.

Set the bowl over a saucepan of gently simmering water—the bottom should at no time be in contact with the water. Do not let the water boil. Whisk the mixture until it is glossy, pale, light, and fluffy and holds a trail when dropped from the whisk. This should take about 5 minutes. Serve immediately in warmed cocktail glasses with ladyfingers for dipping.

Variation To make chilled zabaglione for two: when cooked, remove the bowl from the heat and whisk until completely cold. In a separate bowl, whisk ⅔ cup heavy cream until floppy, then fold into the cold zabaglione. Spoon into glasses and chill for 2–3 hours before serving.

This is one of the best ways of cooking pears. It is simple to make, but tastes luxurious. Use pears that are ripe but not too soft, or they will overcook in the oven. If you can't get a good rich Marsala wine or Vin Santo, use sweet sherry or Madeira.

caramelized pears *with marsala and mascarpone cream*

6 large ripe pears

²/₃ cup caster sugar

²/₃ cup Marsala wine or Vin Santo

8 oz. mascarpone cheese, 1 cup

1 vanilla bean, split, seeds scraped out and reserved

a flameproof, ovenproof pan or dish

serves 6

Cut the pears in half and scoop out the cores—do not peel them. Sprinkle the sugar into the flameproof pan or dish. Set over medium heat and let the sugar melt and caramelize. Remove from the heat as soon as it reaches a medium-brown color and quickly arrange the pears, cut side down, in the caramel.

Bake in a preheated oven at 375°F until the pears are soft, 20–25 minutes. Carefully lift out the pears and transfer to an ovenproof serving dish, keeping the caramel in the pan.

Put the pan on a burner over medium heat and add the Marsala or Vin Santo. Bring to a boil, stirring to dislodge any set caramel, and boil fast until reduced and syrupy. Set aside.

Scoop out a good teaspoon from each cooked pear and put it in a bowl. Add the mascarpone and vanilla seeds and beat well. Fill the centers of the pears with the mascarpone mixture. Return to the oven for 5 minutes until it has heated through. Serve with the caramel sauce spooned over the top.

Ripe figs need almost nothing done to them—but if you bake them with lots of vanilla- and lemon-scented sugar, and hide a walnut in the middle of each one, you will end up with something divine. Take care not to overcook them or they will collapse.

figs baked *with vanilla and lemon*

12 large, fresh ripe figs

12 walnut halves

2 plump vanilla beans

½ cup sugar

grated zest of
1 unwaxed lemon

3 tablespoons white wine

heavy cream or ice cream,
to serve

a shallow ovenproof dish

serves 6

Cut a deep cross in the top of each fig so that they open up a little. Push a walnut half into each cross. Pack the figs closely together in the baking dish.

Chop the vanilla beans and put them in a food processor. Add the sugar and lemon zest and process until the vanilla beans and lemon zest are chopped into tiny bits. Spoon some mixture over each fig and around the dish. Moisten with the white wine.

Bake in a preheated oven at 450°F for 10 minutes until the sugar melts and the figs start to caramelize. Remove from the oven and let cool for a few minutes before serving with cream. Alternatively, serve cold with ice cream.

A refreshing change from the French *tarte au citron*. The almonds give the tart more body and add another flavor dimension. Traditionally, freshly ground almonds are used, because they have a fine, creamy texture and a better flavor than the ready-ground kind.

lemon and almond tart

pasta frolla (pie dough)

2 sticks butter

2 cups all-purpose flour

½ cup sugar

2 egg yolks

lemon and almond filling

4 extra-large eggs, lightly beaten

⅔ cup sugar

finely grated zest and freshly squeezed juice of 3 unwaxed lemons

1 stick unsalted butter, melted

¾ cup sliced almonds, ground to a powder in a blender

whipped cream, to serve

a fluted tart pan, 9 inches diameter

foil and baking beans

a baking tray

serves 8

To make the *pasta frolla*, work the butter into the flour and sugar until it looks like grated Parmesan cheese.

Put the 2 egg yolks in a small bowl, add 1 tablespoon water, and beat lightly. Add to the flour mixture and knead lightly until smooth. Knead into a ball, flatten, then wrap in plastic wrap and let it rest for 30 minutes.

Roll out the dough on a floured surface and use to line the tart pan. Prick the bottom all over with a fork, then chill or freeze it for 15 minutes to set the dough. Line with foil, flicking the edges of the foil inward toward the center so they don't catch on the dough. Fill with baking beans, set on the baking tray and bake blind in the center of a preheated oven at 375°F for 10–12 minutes.

Remove the foil and beans and return the pie crust to the oven for another 5–7 minutes to dry out completely.

To make the filling, put the eggs, sugar, lemon zest, and juice in a bowl and whisk until light and fluffy. Stir in the melted butter and almonds. Mix well and pour into the prepared pie crust. Bake for 25–30 minutes, until the crust and the top of the tart is golden brown. Let cool, then chill before serving with whipped cream.

This amazingly popular dessert is said to have originated in Venice in the 1950s, and is one that actually benefits from being made the day before. For added texture, grind real chocolate in a blender for layering and sprinkling.

tiramisù *with raspberries*

6 oz. semisweet chocolate

8 oz. mascarpone cheese, 1 cup

⅓ cup sugar

6 tablespoons Marsala wine

2 tablespoons dark rum

2 egg yolks

1¼ cups heavy cream, whipped to form soft peaks

½ cup Italian espresso coffee

24 savoiardi or ladyfingers

1 pint fresh raspberries, plus extra to serve

a serving dish or 4 glasses

serves 4 generously

Put the chocolate in a blender or food processor and grind to a powder. Set aside. Put the mascarpone in a bowl and beat in 3 tablespoons sugar, then beat in 2 tablespoons Marsala and the rum. Set aside.

To make the zabaglione mixture, put the egg yolks, 2 tablespoons Marsala, and the remaining 2 tablespoons sugar in a medium heatproof bowl and beat with an electric beater or whisk until well blended. Set the bowl over a saucepan of gently simmering water—the bottom of the bowl should at no time be in contact with the water, and don't let the water boil. Beat the mixture until it is glossy, pale, light, and fluffy and holds a trail when dropped from the whisk, about 5 minutes. Remove the bowl from the heat and whisk until cold. Fold in the whipped cream, then fold in the mascarpone mixture.

Pour the espresso into a bowl and stir in 2 tablespoons Marsala. Dip the savoiardi or ladyfingers, one at a time, into the espresso. Do not leave them in for too long or they will disintegrate. Arrange half the dipped savoiardi in the bottom of a serving dish or 4 glasses. Trickle some more espresso over them, then add a layer of raspberries.

Sprinkle with one-third of the ground chocolate, then spoon half the zabaglione-cream-mascarpone mixture on top. Arrange the remaining dipped savoiardi on top, moisten with any remaining espresso, add some more raspberries, and sprinkle with half the remaining chocolate. Finally spoon the rest of the zabaglione-cream-mascarpone mixture on top and finish with a thick layer of chocolate and a few extra raspberries. Chill in the refrigerator for at least 3 hours (overnight is better) for the flavors to develop. Serve chilled.

amaretti cookies *with pine nuts*

Delicious, crisp little cookies made with a mixture of freshly ground almonds and pine nuts. If you have any peach or apricot kernels, use these in place of some of the almonds and they will impart a fantastic almond flavor to the cookies—in which case, don't add the almond extract. These are wonderful used as the base for a trifle or served with after-dinner liqueurs.

¾ cup blanched almonds

1 cup pine nuts, plus
3 tablespoons extra
for sprinkling

½ cup sugar

2 extra-large egg whites

1 teaspoon almond extract

*a pastry bag fitted with a
plain ½-inch nozzle*

*2 baking trays, lined with
parchment paper*

makes about 30

Put the almonds, pine nuts, and 1 tablespoon of the sugar in a food processor fitted with the grater disk. Grind to a fine powder. Alternatively, use a blender or rotary nut grinder. Set aside.

Put the egg whites in a bowl and beat with an electric beater until stiff but not dry. Gradually beat in the remaining sugar until the whites are stiff and shiny. Fold in the ground nuts and almond extract. Spoon the mixture into the pastry bag and pipe it onto the baking trays in tiny rounds.

Sprinkle with a few extra pine nuts and bake in a preheated oven at 300°F for 30 minutes, until the cookies are lightly browned and hard. Transfer to a wire rack to cool. The cookies may be stored in an airtight container for up to 2 weeks.

These cookies are deliciously buttery and crunchy, and fantastic dipped into Vin Santo or *caffelatte*. These *biscotti* are cooked once in a log, then sliced and cooked again to dry them out. I like to add cornmeal for a slightly gritty texture.

hazelnut and chocolate biscotti

Spread the hazelnuts on a baking tray and toast in a preheated oven at 325°F for 5–10 minutes until they begin to release their aromas. Transfer the hazelnuts to a clean, lintfree dishtowel and rub off the skins. Let cool. Leave the oven on.

Put the butter and sugar in a bowl and beat until pale and creamy. Beat in the egg, vanilla extract, and rum. Using a separate bowl, sift together the flour, cocoa, baking powder, and salt, then stir in the cornmeal. Fold into the butter and egg mixture. Stir in the toasted hazelnuts.

Transfer the dough to a floured counter and knead until smooth. The dough should be soft but not sticky—if it feels sticky, add a little more flour. Divide the dough into 4 pieces. Roll each piece into a log about 2 inches wide and ½ inch high. Flatten them slightly, then put on the prepared baking trays. Bake for 35 minutes or until just golden around the edges.

Let cool slightly then, using a serrated knife, cut diagonally into ½-inch slices. Arrange, cut side down, on the baking trays and bake for another 10–15 minutes until golden brown and crisp. (Take care not to let them burn, or they will taste bitter.) Transfer to a wire rack to cool. Store in an airtight container for up to 1 week.

1⅓ cups whole hazelnuts

1 stick plus 2 tablespoons unsalted butter, softened

1 cup sugar

2 eggs, beaten

2 teaspoon vanilla extract

1 tablespoon dark rum

2 cups all-purpose flour

¾ cup unsweetened cocoa powder

1½ teaspoons baking powder

½ teaspoon salt

½ cup coarse cornmeal

2 baking trays, lined with baking parchment

a wire rack

makes about 30

I have always loved the name of these little chocolate and almond cookies from Piedmont in northern Italy. They are delicious and are often made for special occasions, such as christening teas and weddings.

lady's kisses

1 ½ cups ground almonds, or 2 cups blanched almonds ground in a food processor or blender

a pinch of salt

1 ¼ sticks unsalted butter, at room temperature

1 cup plus 2 tablespoons sugar

1 teaspoon real vanilla extract

⅔ cup all-purpose flour

2 tablespoons unsweetened cocoa powder

chocolate cream

4 oz. semisweet chocolate

⅓ cup heavy cream

2 baking trays, lined with nonstick parchment paper

makes about 24

Put the ground almonds and salt in a bowl and mix well. Put the butter, sugar, and vanilla in a bowl and beat until pale and fluffy. Fold in the ground almonds, sift the flour and cocoa powder over the top, and fold in.

Scoop out teaspoons of mixture and roll into small balls. Arrange the balls on the baking trays allowing room to spread. Press each one to flatten slightly.

Bake in a preheated oven at 350°F for 15 minutes until firm. Remove from the oven, then transfer onto wire racks and let cool.

To make the chocolate cream, put the chocolate and cream in the top of a double boiler over simmering water and heat gently until melted. When melted, remove the top pan and let cool to room temperature. Beat with an electric beater until cold and thick, then chill until firm.

Bring the chocolate cream to room temperature, then use it to sandwich together 2 cookies at a time. Pile up and serve.

This dark, moist chocolate cake is made all over southern Italy, but particularly in Capri. Normally, it is made using ground almonds, but I have adapted this one to suit those who prefer not to eat nuts—it is equally delicious without nuts, and has a fantastic soft texture.

dark chocolate cake

flour, for dusting

7 oz. semisweet chocolate

2 1/2 sticks unsalted butter, softened

1/4 cup espresso coffee

6 eggs, separated

1 cup sugar

scant 1/3 cup potato flour or cornstarch

1/2 teaspoon baking powder

1 cup stale white bread crumbs

confectioners' sugar, for dusting

whipped cream, to serve

a springform cake pan, 10 inches diameter, sides well buttered, bottom lined with nonstick parchment paper

makes 1 cake, 10 inches diameter

Dust the prepared cake pan with flour.

Break up the chocolate and put it in the top of a double boiler. Add the butter. Set it over simmering water and stir occasionally until melted. Remove from the heat, stir in the coffee, then let cool a little.

Put the egg yolks and half the sugar in a bowl and beat until pale and fluffy. Mix in the potato flour and baking powder. Carefully mix in the chocolate and butter mixture, then fold in the bread crumbs.

Put the egg whites in a bowl, beat until stiff but not dry, then gradually beat in the remaining sugar. Gently fold into the chocolate mixture. Pour into the prepared cake pan and bake in a preheated oven at 350°F for about 30 minutes, until risen and almost firm in the center. To test, insert a skewer into the middle of the cake. When removed it should have a little of the mixture clinging to it—this will ensure that the cake is moist. Do not overbake. Invert onto a wire rack to cool. Dust with confectioners' sugar and serve with whipped cream.

Note To make a smaller cake, cut the quantities in half and bake in an 8-inch cake pan.

Fluffy little puffs like this are very popular, and are found in many guises. There is usually one to suit each saint, for his or her particular Saint's Day. Deep-fried snacks like these are part of Italian life and are seen as a real festive treat.

fluffy ricotta fritters

Press the ricotta through a food mill, potato ricer, or a fine mesh strainer into a large bowl. Put the eggs, sugar, and vanilla in a second bowl and whisk until pale and light. Fold into the ricotta.

Sift the flour with the baking powder and salt into a bowl, then fold it into the cheese and egg mixture.

Heat the vegetable oil in the deep-fryer to 375°F. Have a tray lined with paper towels and a slotted spoon or strainer at the ready.

Drop level tablespoons of the mixture into the hot oil in batches of 6. Fry for 2–3 minutes until puffed and deep brown all over (you may have to turn them in the oil). Drain and serve immediately, dusted with confectioners' sugar.

1 cup ricotta cheese

2 eggs, at room temperature

2 tablespoons sugar

1 teaspoon real vanilla extract

¾ cup all-purpose flour

1 teaspoon baking powder

½ teaspoon salt

vegetable oil, for frying

confectioners' sugar, to serve

an electric deep-fryer

a tray lined with paper towels

serves 4–6

basics

classic pesto

2 garlic cloves, peeled

½ cup pine nuts

2 oz. fresh basil leaves without stalks (about 1½ cups)

⅔ cup good olive oil

4 tablespoons unsalted butter, softened

¼ cup freshly grated Parmesan or aged pecorino Romano cheese

sea salt and freshly ground black pepper

serves 4

When made with the freshest of ingredients, this sauce from Liguria is a brilliant green. It can turn a simple bowl of pasta or a piece of cold chicken into a dish that will transport you back to heady summer days.

Classic method Using a mortar and pestle, pound the garlic and pine nuts with a little salt until broken. Add the basil leaves, a few at a time, pounding and mixing to a paste. Gradually beat in the olive oil, little by little, until the mixture is creamy and thick. Beat in the butter and season with pepper, then beat in the cheese. Spoon into a jar with a layer of olive oil on top to exclude the air. Store in the refrigerator until needed, making sure you level the surface each time you use it, and re-cover with olive oil.

For those without much time or a mortar and pestle Put everything in a blender or food processor and process until the pesto is as smooth as you like it to be.

1 large red pepper

2 oz. fresh basil leaves without stalks (about 1½ cups)

1 garlic clove, crushed

2 tablespoons pine nuts, toasted

2 very ripe tomatoes

6 sun-dried tomatoes in oil, drained

3 tablespoons tomato paste

½ teaspoon mild chili powder

½ cup freshly grated Parmesan or aged pecorino Romano cheese

⅔ cup extra virgin olive oil

serves 4

red pesto

Long before red pesto appeared in jars, I made this punchy, robust sauce to remind me of southern Italy. The chili powder is essential, giving a special kick.

Broil the whole pepper, turning until blackened all over. Peel off the skin under running water, cut in half, and remove the stalk and seeds.

Put it in a food processor with the basil, garlic, pine nuts, tomatoes, sun-dried tomatoes, tomato paste, chili powder, and Parmesan, and blend until smooth. With the machine running, slowly pour in the olive oil. Spoon into a jar and cover with a layer of olive oil. This will keep in the refrigerator for up to 2 weeks, topped up with olive oil as you use it.

the pizza maker's tomato sauce

Pizzaiola sauce is named after the traditional sauce that a pizza maker would put on the base of a pizza. It is a specialty of Naples, but common throughout Italy. To acquire its distinctive, concentrated, almost caramelized flavor, the tomatoes must cook at a very lively heat in a shallow pan.

Put the oil in a large, shallow pan and heat almost to smoking point (a wok is good for this). Standing back (it will splutter if it's at the right temperature), add the garlic, oregano, and tomatoes.

Cook over a fierce heat for 5–8 minutes or until the sauce is thick and glossy. Season with salt and pepper.

½ cup olive oil

2 garlic cloves, chopped

1 teaspoon dried (not fresh) oregano

1¾ lb. fresh tomatoes, peeled and coarsely chopped, or two 14½-oz. cans chopped tomatoes

sea salt and freshly ground black pepper

serves 4

béchamel sauce

This creamy sauce is the basis of many comforting pasta dishes, and equally good with meat, vegetable, and fish dishes. The secret is to use more butter than flour, and cook the flour in the butter for at least 5 minutes before adding the milk. To prevent lumps, I take the pan off the heat and add the cold milk all at once, whisking furiously before returning it to the heat to thicken and cook.

Melt the butter in a medium saucepan. When foaming, add the flour and cook over gentle heat for about 5 minutes without letting it brown. Have a balloon whisk ready. Slide the pan off the heat and add all the milk at once, whisking very well. When all the flour and butter have been amalgamated and there are no lumps, return the pan to the heat and slowly bring to a boil, whisking all the time. When it comes to a boil, add salt, simmer gently for 2–3 minutes, then use immediately.

If making in advance, cover the surface directly with plastic wrap to prevent a skin forming, then let cool. When reheating, remove the plastic and reheat very gently, stirring every now and then until liquid. (You may need to whisk it to remove lumps.) If using for lasagne, don't worry too much about lumps—they will disappear when the whole dish cooks. If you like a thinner sauce, just add extra milk after it has boiled and thickened.

6 tablespoons butter

⅓ cup all-purpose flour

about 2 cups milk

sea salt

makes 2 cups

basic pizza dough

1 2/3 cups unbleached all-purpose flour or bread flour, plus extra for sprinkling

1/2 teaspoon salt

1 package active dry yeast (1/4 oz.)

2 tablespoons olive oil

1/2 cup warm water

serves 4

Italian pizza makers use a special flour called tipo 00, available from specialty baking suppliers. If you can't find it, unbleached all-purpose flour or bread flour also make a good base. You can add flavorings such as chopped herbs or grated cheese to the dough, but you may prefer to let the toppings take center stage.

Put the flour, salt, and yeast in a large bowl and mix. Make a well in the center. Add the oil and warm water to the well and gradually work in the flour to make a soft dough. Sprinkle with a little flour if the mixture feels too sticky, but make sure it is not too dry: the dough should be pliable and smooth.

Transfer the dough to a lightly floured counter. Knead for 10 minutes, sprinkling with flour as necessary, until the dough is smooth and elastic.

Rub some oil over the surface of the dough and return the dough to the bowl. Cover with a clean, lintfree dishtowel and leave for about 1 hour, until the dough has doubled in size.

Remove the dough to a lightly floured counter and knead for 2 minutes, until the excess air is knocked out. Roll out the dough according to the recipe you are following.

Nothing beats homemade pasta—not even store-bought "fresh." The texture is silky and the cooked dough itself very light.

fresh egg pasta

1 ⅓ cups all-purpose flour (or use "Italian-style" flour)

a pinch of salt

2 large eggs

1 tablespoon olive oil, plus extra for coating

a pasta machine or rolling pin

serves 2–4

Sift the flour and salt onto a clean counter and make a hollow in the center with your fist. Put the eggs and oil in a bowl, beat well, then pour into the hollow in the flour. Gradually mix the eggs into the flour with the fingers of one hand, and bring it together to form a dough.

Knead the pasta until smooth, lightly massage with a hint of olive oil, put in a plastic bag, and let rest for at least 30 minutes before attempting to roll out. The pasta will be much more elastic after resting. Roll out by hand or machine.

If using a machine, feed the rested dough several times through the widest setting first, folding in 3 each time. Then roll the pasta through all the settings, reducing the settings until reaching the required thickness. Generally the second from last setting is best for tagliatelle, the finest being for ravioli or pasta that is to be filled.

After the required thickness is reached, hang the pasta over a horizontally-fixed broom handle to dry a little—this will make cutting it easier in humid weather, because it will not be so sticky.

Pass the pasta through the chosen cutters, then drape the cut pasta over the broom handle again until ready to cook.

Variation Spinach Pasta *Pasta Verde*

Cook 1 cup frozen spinach according to the package instructions, drain, then squeeze out as much moisture as possible. As for the main recipe, above, sift the flour onto a clean counter and make a hollow in the middle. Put the spinach, 1 extra large egg (instead of 2 large), salt, and pepper in a blender and blend until smooth. Pour this mixture into the hollow in the flour and proceed as in the main recipe, above.

Too many vegetable broths are insipid or taste of a single ingredient. This broth is extravagant in its use of vegetables, but will have very good flavor. Broth gives body and depth of flavor to dishes such as risotto, but shouldn't dominate the dish. Strong root vegetables such as turnips and parsnips are not good additions, and neither are potatoes or cabbage. Remember to wash everything first or you will end up with gritty broth.

vegetable broth

1 large onion, quartered

2 large carrots, quartered

1 small bunch of celery, coarsely chopped (leaves and all)

2 leeks, white parts only, cut in half lengthwise, rinsed, and cut in half again

4 zucchini, thickly sliced

2 tomatoes, cut in half around the middle and seeds squeezed out

1 fennel bulb, quartered

1 romaine lettuce heart, coarsely chopped

3 garlic cloves

1 dried red chile

4 fresh bay leaves

a handful of parsley stalks, crushed

½ lemon, sliced

6 black peppercorns

sea salt, to taste

makes 2–3 quarts

Put all the ingredients in a large soup pot. Add water to cover, about 4 quarts, and bring to a boil. Reduce the heat as soon as it is boiling and simmer for 15 minutes. Stir the broth and skim the surface, then cook at the barest simmer for 1 hour, skimming frequently.

Remove from the heat and strain the broth into a very large bowl through a colander lined with cheesecloth. Discard the contents of the colander after they have cooled. Let the broth cool, then refrigerate for several hours.

At this stage, you can reboil the broth to concentrate it, or cover and refrigerate (or freeze) until needed. The broth will keep in the refrigerator for 3 days or can be frozen for up to 6 months.

index

A
almonds: amaretti cookies 215
    lady's kisses 219
    lemon and almond tart 211
amaretti cookies with pine nuts 215
anchovies: leg of lamb 186
    marinated fresh anchovies 20
    mozzarella in carrozza 39
    pasta with puttanesca sauce 82
    quattro stagioni pizza 112–13
    rosemary and onion *schiacciata* 120
    spinach with pine nuts and 12
    white spaghetti 81
artichokes: artichoke, pesto, and pine nut
    bruschetta 32
    pan-fried artichokes with thyme and
        cool ricotta 135
    quattro stagioni pizza 112–13
arugula: beefsteak with arugula 190
    beetroot, wheat, and arugula salad 128
    cannelloni with ricotta, bitter greens,
        and cherry tomato sauce 78
    grilled fig and prosciutto bruschetta
        with arugula 36
asparagus with egg and truffle butter 11

B
bacon: pasta with carbonara sauce 89
    see also pancetta
basil: classic pesto 226
    red pesto 226
    tomato sauce with double basil 80
béchamel sauce 229
beef: beef braised in red wine 193
    beefsteak with arugula 190
    lasagne al forno 90
beetroot, wheat, and arugula salad 128
bell peppers: grilled tuna steaks with
    peperonata 179
    red pesto 226

roast bell peppers stuffed with pasta
    and tomatoes 138
roasted bell pepper pizza 107
sautéed bell peppers with olives and
    capers 141
bread: creamy tomato and bread soup 42
    focaccia al rosmarino 119
    mozzarella in carrozza 39
    rosemary and onion *schiacciata* 120
    see also bruschetta
bresaola, eggplant pizza with 111
broth, vegetable 234
bruschetta: artichoke, pesto, and pine
    nut 32
    grilled fig and prosciutto with arugula 36
    olive oil and garlic 31
    spicy garlic shrimp on 35
    traditional peasant tomato and garlic 28

C
cake, dark chocolate 220
cannellini beans with olive oil and mint 160
cannelloni with ricotta, bitter greens, and
    cherry tomato sauce 78
cantaloupe melon ice cream 200
caponata 16
caramelized pears 207
carbonara sauce, pasta with 89
carrots with olive oil and Marsala 152
cheese: baked eggplant, tomato,
    mozzarella, and Parmesan 145
    baked polenta with fontina and
        pancetta 93
    creamy radicchio and mascarpone
        risotto 63
    creamy tomato and bread soup 42
    eggplant pizza with bresaola, arugula,
        and Parmesan 111
    fluffy ricotta fritters 223
    Margherita pizza 104
    mozzarella and sun-blushed tomato
        risotto 56
    mozzarella in carrozza 39
    mushroom mezzalune 77

mushroom pizza with basil, chile, and
    garlic oil 108
pan-fried artichokes with thyme and
    cool ricotta 135
Parma ham with figs and balsamic
    dressing 23
Parmesan and butter risotto 55
polenta baked with Italian sausage and
    cheese 97
potato pizza 115
quattro stagioni pizza 112–13
red wine risotto 64
ricotta-stuffed mushrooms 155
roasted bell pepper pizza 107
Roman gnocchi with herbs and
    semolina 98
rosemary and onion *schiacciata* 120
spinach broth with egg and cheese 46
sweet and sour Sicilian eggplant stew 16
zucchini and tomatoes baked with
    fontina 147
chicken: chicken and mushroom risotto 68
    chicken roasted with bay leaves,
        lemon, and garlic 182
chiles: the devil's potatoes 159
    mushroom pizza with basil, chile, and
        garlic oil 108
    pasta with puttanesca sauce 82
chocolate: dark chocolate cake 220
    hazelnut and chocolate biscotti 216
    lady's kisses 219
    tiramisù with raspberries 212
    watermelon sorbetto with chocolate
        chip seeds 203

D
devil's potatoes, the 159
dough: basic pizza 231
    pie 211

E
eggplant: eggplant pizza with bresaola,
    arugula, and Parmesan 111
    baked eggplant, tomato, mozzarella,
        and Parmesan 145

golden eggplant with tomatoes and capers 142

pan-grilled eggplant with lemon, mint, and balsamic vinegar 19

spaghetti with eggplant and tomato sauce 74

sweet and sour Sicilian eggplant stew 16

eggs: asparagus with egg and truffle butter 11

fresh egg pasta 232

pasta with carbonara sauce 89

spinach broth with egg and cheese 46

zabaglione 204

F

fava beans: Sicilian green vegetables 132

fennel and leeks braised in cream and lemon 150

figs: figs baked with vanilla and lemon 208

grilled fig and prosciutto bruschetta 36

Parma ham with figs and balsamic dressing 23

fish: big fish stew 167

fish baked in a salt crust 168

see also individual types of fish

focaccia al rosmarino 119

frisée, orange, and black olive salad 127

fritters: deep-fried sage leaves 24

fluffy ricotta 223

Sicilian chickpea and rosemary 27

zucchini and mint 15

G

gnocchi with herbs and semolina 98

gratin, potato and mushroom 156

H

ham: ham and leek risotto 71

Parma ham with figs and balsamic dressing 23

see also Parma ham

hazelnut and chocolate biscotti 216

I

ice cream, cantaloupe melon 200

Italian mixed salad 124

L

lady's kisses 219

lamb: braised lamb cutlets 185

leg of lamb 186

lasagne al forno 90

leeks: big fish stew 167

fennel and leeks braised in cream and lemon 150

ham and leek risotto 71

lemon: lemon and almond tart 211

marinated fresh anchovies 20

sorbetto al limone 199

lentils braised with little onions and herbs 163

lox: creamy smoked salmon sauce 85

M

Margherita pizza 104

mascarpone: caramelized pears with Marsala and mascarpone cream 207

creamy radicchio and mascarpone risotto 63

tiramisù with raspberries 212

melon: cantaloupe melon ice cream 200

watermelon sorbetto with chocolate chip seeds 203

mint sorbet 200

mozzarella and sun-blushed tomato risotto 56

mozzarella in carrozza 39

mushrooms: chicken and mushroom risotto 68

mushroom mezzalune 77

mushroom pizza with basil, chile, and garlic oil 108

potato and mushroom gratin 156

quattro stagioni pizza 112–13

ricotta-stuffed mushrooms 155

wild mushroom risotto 59

mussels, spaghetti with tomatoes, parsley, and 86

O

oil, basil 42

olive oil and garlic bruschetta 31

olives: orange, frisée, and black olive

salad 127

sautéed peppers with capers and 141

sweet and sour Sicilian eggplant stew 16

onions: braised lamb cutlets with onions, herbs and olives 185

fillets of sole in sweet and sour onion marinade 175

lentils braised with little onions and herbs 163

rosemary and onion schiacciata 120

whole onions baked in their skins 131

orange, frisée, and black olive salad 127

P

pancetta: baked polenta with fontina and pancetta 93

see also bacon

zucchini sautéed with pancetta and thyme 149

pappa al pomodoro 42

Parma ham: mushroom mezzalune 77

with figs and balsamic dressing 23

Parmesan and butter risotto 55

pasta: cannelloni with ricotta, bitter greens, and cherry tomato sauce 78

creamy smoked salmon sauce 85

creamy vodka sauce 89

fresh egg pasta 232

lasagne al forno 90

mushroom mezzalune 77

pasta and bean soup 50

pasta with carbonara sauce 89

pasta with puttanesca sauce 82

roast bell peppers stuffed with pasta and tomatoes 138

spaghetti with eggplant and tomato sauce 74

spaghetti with mussels, tomatoes, and parsley 86

spinach pasta 232

tomato sauce with double basil 80

white spaghetti 81

pears: caramelized pears with Marsala and mascarpone cream 207

peas: Sicilian green vegetables 132

Venetian pea and rice soup 49

pesto: artichoke, pesto, and pine nut bruschetta 32

classic pesto 226

red pesto 226

pie dough 211

pine nuts: amaretti cookies with 215

artichoke, pesto, and pine nut bruschetta 32

classic pesto 226

red pesto 226

spinach with anchovies and 12

pizza maker's tomato sauce 228

pizzas: basic pizza dough 231

eggplant pizza with bresaola, arugula, and Parmesan 111

Margherita pizza 104

marinara pizza 103

mushroom pizza with basil, chile, and garlic oil 108

potato pizza 115

quattro stagioni pizza 112–13

roasted bell pepper pizza 107

polenta: baked polenta with fontina and pancetta 93

polenta baked with Italian sausage and cheese 97

soft polenta with sausage ragù 94

pork loin roasted with rosemary and garlic 189

potatoes: devil's potatoes, the 159

Italian mixed salad 124

potato and mushroom gratin 156

potato pizza 115

prosciutto: Parma ham with figs and balsamic dressing 23

prosciutto and fig bruschetta 36

puttanesca sauce, pasta with 82

Q

quattro stagioni pizza 112–13

R

radicchio: creamy radicchio and mascarpone risotto 63

potato pizza 115

ragù 90, 94

raspberries, tiramisù with 212

ribollita, la 45

rice: chicken and mushroom risotto 68

creamy radicchio and mascarpone risotto 63

ham and leek risotto 71

mozzarella and sun-blushed tomato risotto 56

Parmesan and butter risotto 55

red wine risotto 64

seafood and saffron risotto 67

spring risotto with herbs 60

Venetian pea and rice soup 49

wild mushroom risotto 59

ricotta: cannelloni with ricotta, bitter greens, and cherry tomato sauce 78

fluffy ricotta fritters 223

pan-fried artichokes with thyme and cool ricotta 135

ricotta-stuffed mushrooms 155

risotto *see* rice

Roman gnocchi 98

rosemary: *focaccia al rosmarino* 119

rosemary and onion *schiacciata* 120

Sicilian chickpea and rosemary fritters 27

S

sage leaves, deep-fried 24

salsa, caper and mint 176

sardines baked with garlic, lemon, olive oil, and breadcrumbs 171

sauces: béchamel 229

classic pesto 226

creamy smoked salmon 85

creamy vodka 89

pizza maker's tomato 228

red pesto 226

tomato with double basil 80

sausages: grilled sausages with tomato and sage bean stew 194

polenta baked with Italian sausage and cheese 97

soft polenta with sausage ragù 94

schiacciata, rosemary and onion 120

sea bass baked in parchment 172

seafood and saffron risotto 67

semolina, Roman gnocchi with herbs and 98

shrimp, spicy garlic 35

Sicilian eggplant stew 16

Sicilian chickpea and rosemary fritters 27

Sicilian green vegetables 132

smoked salmon sauce 85

sole fillets in sweet and sour onion marinade 175

sorbets: mint sorbet 200

sorbetto al limone 199

watermelon sorbetto with chocolate chip seeds 203

spaghetti: spaghetti with eggplant and

tomato sauce 74

spaghetti with mussels, tomatoes, and parsley 86

white spaghetti 81

spinach: spinach broth with egg and cheese 46

spinach pasta 232

spinach with anchovies and pine nuts 12

spring risotto with herbs 60

sweet and sour Sicilian eggplant stew 16

T
tarts: lemon and almond tart 211

tomato upside-down tart 116

tiramisù with raspberries 212

tomatoes: baked eggplant, tomato, mozzarella, and Parmesan 145

big fish stew 167

cannelloni with ricotta, bitter greens, and cherry tomato sauce 78

creamy tomato and bread soup 42

golden eggplant with tomatoes and capers 142

grilled sausages with tomato and sage bean stew 194

grilled tuna steaks with peperonata 179

Margherita pizza 104

marinara pizza 103

mozzarella and sun-blushed tomato risotto 56

mozzarella in carrozza 39

pasta with puttanesca sauce 82

pizza maker's tomato sauce 228

quattro stagioni pizza 112–13

red pesto 226

roast bell peppers stuffed with pasta and tomatoes 138

roasted bell pepper pizza 107

slow-roasted tomatoes with garlic and oregano 137

soft polenta with sausage ragù 94

spaghetti with eggplant and tomato sauce 74

spaghetti with mussels, tomatoes, and parsley 86

spicy garlic shrimp with tomatoes and chickpeas 35

sweet and sour Sicilian eggplant stew 16

tomato sauce with double basil 80

tomato upside-down tart 116

traditional peasant tomato and garlic bruschetta 28

zucchini and tomatoes baked with fontina 147

tuna: grilled tuna steaks with peperonata 179

oven-baked tuna with salsa 176

V
vegetable broth 234

Venetian pea and rice soup 49

vodka sauce, creamy 89

W
watermelon sorbetto with chocolate chip seeds 203

wheat, beetroot, and arugula salad 128

white spaghetti 81

wine: beef braised in red wine 193

caramelized pears with Marsala and mascarpone cream 207

carrots with olive oil and Marsala 152

mint sorbet 200

red wine risotto 64

zabaglione 204

Z
zabaglione 204

zucchini: zucchini and mint fritters 15

zucchini and tomatoes baked with fontina 147

zucchini sautéed with pancetta and thyme 149

conversion charts

Weights and measures have been rounded up or down slightly to make measuring easier.

Volume equivalents:

American	Metric	Imperial
1 teaspoon	5 ml	
1 tablespoon	15 ml	
1/4 cup	60 ml	2 fl.oz.
1/3 cup	75 ml	2 1/2 fl.oz.
1/2 cup	125 ml	4 fl.oz.
2/3 cup	150 ml	5 fl.oz. (1/4 pint)
3/4 cup	175 ml	6 fl.oz.
1 cup	250 ml	8 fl.oz.

Weight equivalents: Measurements:

Imperial	Metric	Inches	Cm
1 oz.	25 g	1/4 inch	5 mm
2 oz.	50 g	1/2 inch	1 cm
3 oz.	75 g	3/4 inch	1.5 cm
4 oz.	125 g	1 inch	2.5 cm
5 oz.	150 g	2 inches	5 cm
6 oz.	175 g	3 inches	7 cm
7 oz.	200 g	4 inches	10 cm
8 oz. (1/2 lb.)	250 g	5 inches	12 cm
9 oz.	275 g	6 inches	15 cm
10 oz.	300 g	7 inches	18 cm
11 oz.	325 g	8 inches	20 cm
12 oz.	375 g	9 inches	23 cm
13 oz.	400 g	10 inches	25 cm
14 oz.	425 g	11 inches	28 cm
15 oz.	475 g	12 inches	30 cm
16 oz. (1 lb.)	500 g		
2 1b.	1 kg		

Oven temperatures:

110°C	(225°F)	Gas 1/4
120°C	(250°F)	Gas 1/2
140°C	(275°F)	Gas 1
150°C	(300°F)	Gas 2
160°C	(325°F)	Gas 3
180°C	(350°F)	Gas 4
190°C	(375°F)	Gas 5
200°C	(400°F)	Gas 6
220°C	(425°F)	Gas 7
230°C	(450°F)	Gas 8
240°C	(475°F)	Gas 9

credits

All the recipes featured in this book are by Maxine Clark except the following, which are by Silvana Franco:

Basic Pizza Dough
Creamy Smoked Salmon Sauce
Creamy Vodka Sauce
Eggplant with Bresaola, Arugula, and Parmesan
Marinara Pizza
Mushroom Mezzalune
Mushroom Pizza with Basil, Chile, and Garlic Oil
Pasta with Carbonara Sauce
Pasta with Puttanesca Sauce
Quattro Stagioni Pizza
Roasted Bell Pepper Pizza
Tomato Sauce with Double Basil
White Spaghetti

Photographs

Martin Brigdale
Pages 2, 10, 17, 21, 22, 43, 44, 47, 48, 51, 53 center, 53 right, 54, 57, 58, 61, 62, 65, 66, 69, 70, 72, 75, 87, 91, 92, 95, 99, 101 center, 101 right, 105, 114, 117, 118, 125, 126, 144, 164, 165 left, 165 right, 166, 173, 174, 178, 181 center, 181 right, 184, 191, 195, 197 left, 198, 205, 210, 213, 222, 227, 229, 235, 237

Peter Cassidy
Front endpaper left, 13, 14, 18, 24, 40, 41 center, 41 right, 53 left, 73 left, 73 right, 79, 96, 100, 101 left, 121, 123 all, 129, 130, 133, 134, 136–137, 139, 140, 143, 146–147, 148, 151, 153, 154, 157, 158, 161, 162, 165 center, 169, 170, 177, 182–183, 187, 188, 192, 196, 206–207, 209, 217, 225 all, 238

William Lingwood
Pages 9 center, 73 center, 76, 80, 81, 83, 84–85, 86, 88–89, 102–103, 106, 109, 110–111, 112–113, 138, 145, 180, 211, 228, 230–231, 232–233

Gus Filgate
Pages 8, 9 left, 25, 26, 29, 30, 33, 34, 37, 38, 122

Jean Cazals
Pages 201, 202, 203, 214, 218, 221

James Merrell
Pages 11, 135, 181 left, 224

Chris Tubbs
Front endpaper right, pages 3, 7

Alan Williams
Pages 6, 199, 240

Francesca Yorke
Pages 9 right, 197 center, 197 right

Nicky Dowey
Pages 30, 64

David Munns
Pages 52, 107

Pia Tryde
Back endpaper right, page 4

Caroline Arber
Page 98

Christopher Drake
Back endpaper left

David Loftus
Page 5

Debi Treloar
Page 1

Ian Wallace
Page 41 left